Dark Side of Digital Organizations

İlkay Öztürk (ed.)

Dark Side of Digital Organizations

PETER LANG

Bibliographic Information published by the Deutsche Nationalbibliothek
The Deutsche Nationalbibliothek lists this publication in the Deutsche Nationalbibliografie; detailed bibliographic data is available online at http://dnb.d-nb.de.

Library of Congress Cataloging-in-Publication Data
A CIP catalog record for this book has been applied for at the Library of Congress.

This publication was printed with the support of Bahçeşehir Üniversitesi.

Cover illustration: © ipopba/stock.adobe.com

ISBN 978-3-631-83110-6 (Print)
E-ISBN 978-3-631-84141-9 (E-PDF)
E-ISBN 978-3-631-84142-6 (EPUB)
E-ISBN 978-3-631-84143-3 (MOBI)
DOI 10.3726/b17827

Peter Lang – Berlin · Bern · Bruxelles · New York · Oxford · Warszawa · Wien

This publication has been peer reviewed.

www.peterlang.com

I would like to thank my colleague Prof Dr H. Okan Yeloğlu for his support in the creation of the book's concept.

Contents

List of Figures

List of Tables

Introduction

Digital transformation, if applied correctly, is a true competitive weapon for organizations. Digital transformation increases revenues; it increases customer satisfaction and triggers innovation by transforming business processes and models. However, if business functions such as management, human resources, logistics and finance cannot manage digital transformation well, there may be a danger of extinction for companies. In the coming periods, business life will continue to be affected by digital transformation. In this long journey, it is necessary to consider digital transformation as a moving target, a strategy that is constantly evolving, changing and needs to be updated. For this reason, businesses that have not yet implemented their digital transformation strategies or are still doing so need to know the challenges they will face in digital transformation. In the book, we tried to address the dark points that businesses should pay attention to rather than the benefits of digital transformation. That's why we've named the book as the dark side of digital organizations.

In the first chapter, the teleworking model, which is one of the flexible working models that accelerates with digital transformation, is explained. The problems related to the physical, psychological, employee commitment and perceived roles that employees working from home may encounter were explained. Employers' performance measurement problems related to the telework system, the career development of the employee and the problems that may be experienced with the organizational culture were presented and information was given about what managers should do to ensure a home-based working culture.

In the second chapter, the challenges of working in an IT-focused environment are explained in order for human resource management to cope with the changes occurring in digital organizations. In this section, information about e-human resources functions such as e-personnel affairs and e-payrolling, e-planning, e-recruitment and e-selection, e-training, e-performance management, e-remuniration and e-career management has been given, and difficulties have been discussed, and problems to be overcome are presented.

In the third chapter, information management problems in the digital world are discussed today, where information is considered an important strategic resource and power. In this chapter, points to be considered by digital organizations when managing information and the dark side of information management are presented.

The fourth chapter discusses how businesses relate to digital strategies while identifying new business models to sustain the pressures and visions that digitalization creates to change business strategies. Since digital developments force organizations to produce an aggression strategy, the phenomenon of digital strategy has been explored on the axis of the dark side of digitalization and the scope of digital disruption has been discussed.

In the fifth chapter, the threats posed by Digital Financial Process Transformation to organizations are discussed. With the addition of mobile Internet and Internet of Things to rapidly changing financial systems with artificial intelligence, blockchain and cloud technology, it has become difficult to achieve financial stability.

In the sixth chapter, changing organizational structures in digital transformation, difficulties in communication, coordination and management processes are discussed in the management dimension. Issues that should be taken into consideration by managers and leaders, such as work-life balance, occupational diseases, technology addiction, the image and brand value of the company, which has deteriorated due to cyberattacks, were pointed out.

In the seventh chapter, in the context of digitalized business processes, the problems encountered in the digitalization of third party logistics service providers, which are among the main components of the supply chain, are discussed. Problems in the supply chain and logistics services due to customs regulations and tariffs, legal regulations, natural disasters and epidemics, non-integrated business processes and delayed investments, cyber security threats, organizational culture and employee motivation have been revealed.

İlkay Öztürk

1. DARK SIDE OF TELEWORKING

Abstract The breaking points of human history as it passed from primitive societies to the information society have changed the production systems and consequently the forms of employment. The digital revolutions experienced after the Industrial Revolution also transformed the way of doing business. This transformation has enabled people to work remotely with the help of technology, without having to be physically present at the workplace. Our aim in this section is to reveal the drawbacks, difficulties and disadvantages of working from home, which is one of the flexible working types, in terms of employees and employers.

Keywords: *flexible working model, teleworking, working from home, disadvantages of teleworking*

With increase in production and start of migration with the invention of the steam engine in the 1800s Industry 1.0, with the beginning of mass production using electricity at the beginning of the twentieth century Industry 2.0, with the inclusion of computers in production at the end of the twentieth century and the start of production robots to work more effectively and faster than humans Industry 3.0 and at the beginning of the twenty-first century, with the minimum level of human participation in production and production using artificial intelligence and the Internet of Things (IoT) Industry 4.0 has entered to our lives. The labor based on muscle power needed in the First Industrial Revolution turned into labor based on brain power in the information society. This transformation has enabled people to work remotely with the help of technology, without having to be physically present at the workplace.

This model, which is called flexible working model, provides the opportunity to determine the working places and hours according to the needs, depending on the agreement between the employee and the employer. There are many types of flexible working model that started to be implemented in the 1970s. However, a model whose conditions are not well defined can lead to inefficiency for both employees and employers in the long term. Working from home model, which is generally preferred voluntarily, can be compulsory in some cases. We have all experienced that the world faced pandemic threat in 2020, and many businesses had to be resumed from home. Here, it was not possible to achieve the same success in every sector, but sectors with strong technological infrastructure and companies that could motivate their employees even from a distance and increase their psychological resilience were able to manage their business successfully. For this reason, it is necessary to rearrange the work and family life of the individual and to determine the physical, psychological and temporal boundaries in order to increase productivity and success.

1.1 Border (Boundary) Theory

With the industrial revolution, production was concentrated in a single center, i.e., in factories, in other words "at work." This process, which initially started as a physical change, brought about emotional, intellectual and behavioral changes over time. After the Industrial Revolution, workplace and home started to differ from each other in terms of purpose and culture. Based on this fact, Clark developed the work/family border theory. The foundation of the theory is based on Kurt Lewin's idea that "living spaces" (psychological environment in which each individual lives; "work" and "family") create different areas or environments that affect each other. According to Clark, boundaries are border lines that define the starting and ending point of the behavior associated with the area. These boundaries are divided into three as physical, temporal and psychological. The physical boundary defines where space-related behavior will take place, such as the walls of the workplace or the walls of the house. Temporal boundaries, such as working hours, determine when family responsibilities will be fulfilled or work will be done.

Psychological boundaries are the rules which are created by individuals to determine whether thought patterns, behavioral patterns and emotions are appropriate for an area (Clark, 2000: 756). According to Clark (2000: 748), people are "border passers" who make daily transitions between two worlds (business and family).

People staying in the business and home area are called "border guards" or "area members." Children and spouse at home are border guardians/area members. In the workplace, managers and colleagues are border guards/area members. Family pictures, telephones from home, etc. in the work area and work brought home, customer phones, etc. in the home area are called "permeable." Boundary theory places the individual at the center as an active subject, and has developed an important approach in this respect. Technology today has led to significant changes in the way people work; organizations without borders, virtual workplaces and the ability to provide continuous wireless connection to one's work have been the means of this change (Kreiner et al.,

2009: 704). Boundary theory can be used effectively to determine the psychological boundaries of the individual in a process where boundaries are physically eliminated and work relations undergo great transformations.

1.2 Flexible Working Models

The concept of flexibility does not mean an environment of freedom where employers can employ workers as they wish. Employers need to acknowledge that flexibilization is a way of dealing with fluctuations in labor supply and demand. According to Pollerts (1988), flexibility means less regulation, reduction of rules, and facilitation for employers in hiring and firing.

Flexible working models are defined by International Labour Organization (ILO) as follows (Kaya and Doğan, 2016: 1071).

- Part-Time Work: It is less work in working time, which is formed by mutual agreements between the employee and the employer. Part-time work is a work with a reduced duration. Duration differs from country to country. Part-time work is continuous and it is separated from short-term work with this element.
- Job Sharing: A full-time job is carried out by a few people in turn at certain times of the day. Split day, split week, and alternating week shapes are available.
- Flexible (Flexible) Work Periods: It is the determination of the length of the daily working period of the workers by themselves, on the condition that they work compulsorily at a basic time. This basic time is expressed as "actual, constant or core time." The employee comes to work whenever he/she wants outside of this core period, and determines his/her break.
- Working on the Call: There are two types. In the first, the parties determine how long the worker will work within the zone. The work period when the worker will fulfill is specified by the call. In the second type, the right to determine belongs entirely to the employer. The basis of this operating model is the need to ensure the business adapts to demand changes by providing flexibility to the business.

Apart from these, in the models such as Intensive Work Week, Flexible Shift and Flexible Transition to Retirement, the working place of the employees is the workplace, while in the Home Work and Telework models, unlike the others, working is done at home."

1.3 The Concept of Teleworking

Teleworking concept is a work arrangement in which employees work at home, not at work, during working hours. According to this regulation, the work of the employees is carried to the home environment. This work can be done during or outside normal working hours. Telework is a subcategory of the broader concept of remote work. It includes workers who use information and communications technology (ICT) or landline telephones to carry out the work remotely (ILO, 2020: 6)

In literature, virtual work is also used instead of teleworking. Teleworking (virtual work) and remote work should not be confused with each other. Virtual work is the work of employees from their homes using computers and Internet instead of offices. Gray et al. (1995) identify those who work remote for much of the working day as full-time homeworkers, sometimes attending an office for meetings or gathering information. In this group suited engineers and programmers, system administrators, telephone order agents and data entry clerks are included. (Hobbs & Armstrong, 1998: 366).

On the other hand; remote work is a form of work in which employees work in workplaces called head offices, but spend at least half of their working time outside of this head office (Acar and Acar, 2019:). Drivers working under logistics companies, medical representatives of pharmaceutical companies and salespeople meeting with customers face to face are included in this group. Employees do not usually work at home regularly but instead, work in the workplace on one or two full workdays a week. The remaining days will be spent in the workplace (Lim and Teo, 2000: 561).

Teleworking is also often confused with "working at home." Working at home is the form of work performed by the employee in his own home, but without employer supervision, as required by the employment contract. The majority of the working at home is household production which is carried out within the informal sector, by unskilled labor, without any security and with low wages. It is a working model generally applied in the textile industry.

1.4 Effects of Teleworking

The COVID-19 virus, which emerged in 2020 and has a very high risk of transmission, has caused jobs in many sectors around the world to be done from home at various levels. People have developed protective measures called social distance to reduce the contagiousness of the virus and have had to comply with these measures both in their social and business lives. (Fadinger and

Schymik, 2020). The social distance rule has forced people to work from home. Teleworking, which was considered as a flexible working in the past, is used as a mandatory method to protect the health of the society in this period (Dockery and Bawa, 2020). The increase in teleworking has also increased digitalization. Applications such as Zoom, Adobe connect, Microsoft Teams and Slack, which tens of millions of people use for business meetings and interviews, have become platforms used by hundred millions with the inclusion of education. Information and communication technologies have developed very rapidly in this period. While people are working from home, they have started to conduct their meetings and interviews through digital applications. In this context, countries have developed similar applications and software programs to compete. Lessons, meetings, exams can be done through these applications, concerts can be given and museums can be visited using digital applications (Dockery and Bawa, 2020; Gupta, 2020: 1). During the COVID-19 pandemic period, many advantages of working from home have been identified:

For employees:

- Employees' performance may increase as time spent in traffic and on the road and leisure time at work is saved.
- Employees can spare the time they will waste to go to work for their children and families. They may feel more energetic because they will be less tired.

For employers:

- Various expenses such as transportation, food, fuel, stationery expenses, energy use for the employee can be reduced (Dockery and Bawa, 2020).

These advantages can turn into disadvantages if remote work is not well planned and managed to provide the desired performance. Working from home also has a number of disadvantages. For example, the inability of employees to meet face to face, lack of sufficient technological infrastructure, deterioration of work-life balance are some of these. In a study conducted with 1,014 participants, 56 % of the employees stated that they were less productive by working from home (Rubin et al., 2020: 4). Many problems related to working from home can reduce the productivity of the employee.

Fig. 1.1 shows the percentages of advantages and disadvantages of working from home that affect employees. According to the research conducted by Rubin et al. (2020), homeworkers experience problems such as increasing tasks at home, decreasing social interaction with colleagues, deterioration of work-life balance, inability to focus, inability to create ergonomics in the workplace, and inadequate technology and equipment.

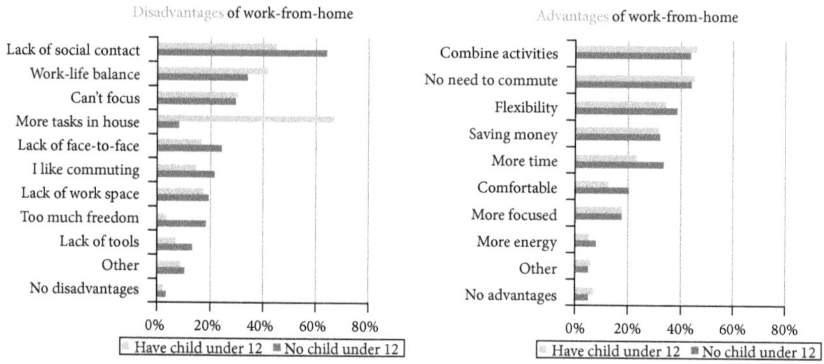

Fig. 1.1: Perceived advantages and disadvantages of working from home (%) (Rubin et al., 2020: 5).

1.4.1 Effects on the Physical Environment

Organizing the environment in the workplace is a responsibility of the employer and is designed according to the working conditions. However, employees may not be able to design their home environments in the same way. Teleworkers must be able to get ready to work without oversight. Having space at home to set up computers and other equipment is needed. Anyone employed at home would also need to find the flexibility to cope with defects with equipment without the back-up that will be required in an office. Employers save on space, heating and lighting and the total efficiency is greatly increased. It will attract professional workers by giving them more flexible working arrangements, including teleworking. The drawbacks for employers may include difficulties in installing and maintaining suitable equipment at different sites, as well as the potential for poor coordination between employers and teleworkers. Most employers do not bear the necessary costs to turn the home environment into a "home office" for these and similar reasons (Harrison, 2001: 5). Therefore, the employee has to provide this physical environment with his/her own means.

However, it is found that the home office is not always the most convenient place to work, even if the job itself was conducive to telework, particularly when other members of the household have to recall. For example, certain participants might identify other family members who are at home during the day, reducing their work time to the evenings or weekends (Bentley and Yoong, 2000: 352).

It is very important that homeworkers ensure their own discipline. Those who work from home should be at the desk at their own time. They should connect their working time to their routine. This can increase their productivity. There are more distractions at home than at work. For example, postponing the work they have to do and starting housework, socializing, watching television, taking care of your child, spending a long time for private phone calls are some of these. In order to avoid these distractions, it is necessary to use a room in the house as an office, to focus on work while in this room, and to explain this awareness to other family members in the house. Thus, while the employee is in the home office, communication with other family members will be reduced and distractions will be ignored.

1.4.2 Psychological Effects

The inconveniences of becoming a teleworker are largely psychological to the person. Individuals in certain teleworking settings can be totally excluded from collective touch. This may be either by their own choices, as in the case of a writer or poet who retires to the mountains to compose alone, or by chance. In the latter case, the only contact with others may be by infrequent e-mail messages detailing directives, and it is in such situations where the effects of social isolation on the person are likely to be severe (Hobbs and Armstrong, 1998: 367). Social and professional isolation caused by employees' distancing from their colleagues, interruption of informal news flows in the workplace, not being aware of new developments and decisions taken increase the feeling of loneliness and employees may experience internal tension.

The technical advances still come at an expense. Researchers also observed that employees face different forms of work-related stress in teleworking environments where contact and engagement rely on information technology (IT) (Suh and Lee, 2017: 153). Employees who have long been involved in face-to-face job processes have heightened job tension because they have to deal with sudden and profound shifts in the design of work conditions and are expected to keep pace with technical developments. Such IT-caused work tension is called "technostress" and is seen as an impediment to job satisfaction for teleworkers (Srivastava et al., 2015: 356)

The fact that the employee's home and business life is in the same environment causes them to live their lives routinely. After a while, this routine can lead to not being excited about the work done, not being able to focus on the work and eventually having psychological problems.

1.4.3 Career Development and Its Effect on Wages

One of the most important problems of working from home is that it causes loss of status and negatively affects career development (Hobbs and Armstrong, 1998: 367). The opportunities provided by the employer are important for the career development of the employees. Wages, social benefits, personal rights affect the career development of employees. However, if employers encourage employees to work from home in order not to give these rights to employees, it is unethical behavior. Unfortunately, many employers pay less to homeworkers. And he prefers this method especially. For example, there is a 4/5 wage difference between women working part-time and full-time in the UK. This ratio is 2/3 among men. This shows that some arrangements can be made against the employee in terms of social rights and wages when working from home. Since homeworkers are away from each other both physically and in terms of solidarity, their loyalty to the workplace decreases and layoffs can be easier because they can be de-unionized. This situation causes the employees working from home to be unable to make career plans and their future to be uncertain. This causes inequality of opportunity among employees (Koçak and Kavi, 2010: 83).

Employees feel that their reduced physical presence in the workplace will have a negative impact on business development and opportunities for success. Consequently, many workers, particularly those holding technical positions are reluctant to embrace teleworking (Lim and Teo, 2000: 567). Employees in the workplace can gain more experience in their work by developing mutual and continuous relationships, brainstorm and their careers can develop in this direction, but homeworkers fear that they will be deprived of promotions or awards as their visibility in the workplace decreases and their relationship with their managers decreases. At the same time, because they cannot brainstorm how to get the job done, they may go wrong or finish it longer. This negatively affects their career development.

1.4.4 Effects on Organizational Commitment

Working from home can also reduce organizational commitment and the ability to learn and adopt organizational culture, as it promotes autonomy rather than solidarity. Failure to work in the center of the business will prevent the sharing of organizational culture by all employees. In this context, organizational commitment of the employee who works from home may decrease (Topcuk, 2006: 39).

Workers with lower organizational commitment develop a more appropriate teleworking attitude. The possible reason for this result is that persons with low levels of interpersonal engagement would choose to separate themselves from the organization physically, rather than function at home (Lim and Teo, 2000: 567). Some studies have identified numerous factors that may impede the happiness of teleworkers, such as physical and social alienation and the absence of an organizational sense of belonging. These studies generally indicate that teleworkers are concerned about being excluded from decision-making and considered less loyal to their working community, which causes them to rely heavily on ITs to signal their presence and minimize their sense of social alienation in the remote workplace to a greater extent than they do when they work in an office (Suh and Lee, 2017: 153).

1.4.5 Effects on Perceived Roles

One of the difficulties of working from home is related to the perceived role and working environment. Especially homeworkers may find it difficult to allocate the appropriate amount of time for work and home activities. Again, maintaining self-discipline and being motivated can be difficult (Lim and Teo, 2000: 567; Mills et al., 2001: 52).

Employees largely decide where and when they will work, but this flexibility causes an imbalance between work and non-work roles (Naswall et al., 2008: 5). Work and family roles prepare the ground for conflicts. Especially the fact that female employees have to assume roles such as mother, wife, working woman together in the same environment increases the conflict.

Unethical behavior may also cause employees to have role conflicts. For example, employers may tend to give more work to homeworkers by saying "somehow he works at home, I will give him the most work." This situation may force the employee to work more and cause conflict between their private life and their roles in business life. Especially, employees with low emotional intelligence cannot manage this situation. The employee, who spends more time with his wife and children, delays his job. Delayed jobs can lead to layoffs (Koçak and Kavi, 2010: 84).

1.4.6 Effects on Job Satisfaction

Working from home causes stress on employees called technostressors. Technostressors are sourced from technology characteristics (existence (or in existence) of IT and changing IT technologies) and job characteristics (job autonomy and task interdependence). It is known that stress factors in technology and job characteristics cause decreases in job satisfaction.

Research from Suh and Lee (2017) has shown that mission interdependence has an additive impact on a strain by increasing work burden and privacy invasion, whereas job autonomy has decreased strain by decreasing privacy invasion. Second, job pressure, privacy violation, and role uncertainty are the major causes of the burden on teleworkers. Third, technology and work dynamics underlying cycles, technostressors and pressure differ depending on IoT. The findings suggest that stressors caused by technology (i.e., task pressure, privacy violation, and uncertainty of role) contribute to a greater burden, which in turn decreases job satisfaction for teleworkers (Suh and Lee, 2017: 153).

If the way of working from home increases the routine of the employee and employees cannot use their creativity, alienation begins. This is an important problem in organizational life. Dissatisfaction begins in employees who become alienated from their jobs. The more the employees use their creativity in their work, the more they enjoy it and the work becomes fun. (Koçak and Kavi, 2010: 85).

1.4.7 Effects on Performance Measurement

Since managers cannot physically observe the performance of homeworkers, they may not be able to discover their strengths and weaknesses. This may lead to management results such as not being able to fully measure their performance, not being able to give confidence, not being able to audit, and not be able to make correct evaluation (Lim and Teo, 2000: 569; Ward and Shabha, 2001: 68).

All the difficulties listed for homeworkers; institutional difficulties, hardening of teamwork, weakening of relations with managers, restriction of opportunities, and insufficiency of technological resources may cause employees to underperform. Even if the employee's performance is good, because of the difficulties in monitoring and measuring the performance of the employees, teleworking cannot be easily adapted to the corporate structure. Therefore, organizations should clearly state how the performance of homeworkers will be measured. Homeworkers who know how to measure their performance can work more comfortably psychologically.

1.4.8 Effects on Organizational Culture

Organizational culture is a paradigm that provides information about the organization. Organizational culture guides employees on how to behave in the organization. It increases their ability to know how to solve problems and how processes will work.

Each company possesses its own distinctive culture. The organizational culture, consisting of written or unwritten laws, beliefs and values, brings together individuals with different views, beliefs and values around a common purpose and thus helps the organization achieve its goals (Ozcan and Oztürk, 2020: 46). However, when working remotely, managers may have problems in conveying organizational culture to employees who are physically distant because learning is provided not only in a formal way but also in an informal way among employees such as in breaks, lunches, corridors (Bailey and Kurland, 1999; 59–60).

Organizations must create a new culture for the way to work from home and ensure that homeworkers adapt to this culture. Here, the leader of the organization has a great responsibility. The digital leadership concept, which is one of the most discussed among leadership styles recently, is the most needed way of working from home.

1.4.9 Effects on Job Security and Data Security

Since the incremental reduction in data transmission costs and tremendous improvements in speed and power have resulted in an increase in the affordability and accessibility of personal computers which enable people to work at home (Teo et al., 1998: 329).

Employers may experience data security issues when working from home. The problem of getting into the hands of third parties, being used by other organizations, being lost or deliberately destroying the information that needs to be private and confidential to the organization involves a threat in terms of data security (Mills et al., 2001: 52).

Information technologies pose a threat to the privacy of individuals because they store many data in different environments. Although employers take security measures in the workplace, these measures may not be valid when employees work in different locations due to network connections. The dissemination of information sent over the network on different platforms or being seen by other people at home can cause ethical problems for the organization. Licensed software installed on computers at work could not be installed on home computers, which could endanger data security (Guthrie, 1997: 3).

At the same time, if we evaluate the issue in terms of occupational safety, the employer is obliged to protect all employees against work accidents and occupational diseases. However, living these accidents or illnesses at home can lead to uncertainty about whether they are covered by insurance or not.

Likewise, the increase in working from home has led to an increase in home accidents. Employees who cannot create an ergonomically suitable environment at home are most likely to suffer from musculoskeletal diseases. Especially during the 2020 pandemic, the curfews limited their daily activities. Some businesses supported their employees with online exercise programs in this process (Bouziri et al., 2020: 510).

1.4.10 Social Effects

Working from home can also have negative social consequences. Working from home can damage a person's ability to relate to other people. In this case, it can affect the quality of the social relationship in an uncomfortable and undesirable way (Mills et al., 2001: 529). At the same time, individuals working from home may be perceived as not working by their neighbors in societies where professions are seen as social status. In some cultures, gender roles are shared by society. The social status of male individuals working at home can be damaged, especially in societies where men work outside and are obliged to look after their family.

1.5 Works Suitable for Teleworking

While many jobs can be done from home today, some jobs require employees to physically come to the workplace. In this process, organizations need to decide which works will be carried out from home and which works will be carried out from the workplace.

However, there is no research done in the last decade to dig at in specific the teleworking efficiency. According to the survey results conducted in 2020 with 1964 adults in USA, as many as 26 % of employees favored the idea of work from home and would continue to pursue it, although more than 38 % chose the mix of work in the workplace, while the others suggest not being happy with teleworking (Irawanto, 2020: 166).

There is a positive correlation between highly skilled professions such as education, finance, insurance, real estate, e-commerce, banking and the opportunity to work from home. However, in sectors such as agriculture, construction, food, procurement, fisheries, retail, distribution, security and healthcare sectors, the potential of individuals to work from home is very low. The opportunity to work remotely is higher for those who have a high level of education, have permanent employment contracts, and those who work in urban areas and large enterprises (Meltem and Küçükoğlu, 2020: 76). While those with most

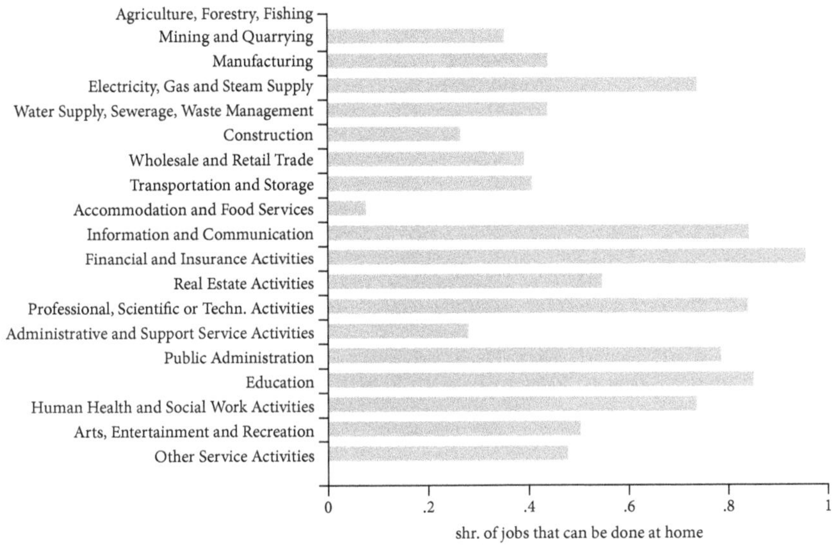

Fig. 1.2: Share of jobs that can be performed at home. Notes: The figure plots the estimated shares of jobs that can be done at home in the German economy across broad NACE Rev. 2 industries (Fadinger and Schymik, 2020: 3).

of the income distribution will be able to work from home, those who are at the bottom of the income distribution have little potential to work from home (Fadinger and Schymik, 2020: 3). Fig. 1.2 shows the estimated share of home jobs in the German economy.

Similarly, according to the research of Deloitte (2020) conducted in Turkey, the media, advertising, service, technology, e-commerce, energy and education sectors are at the top of remote working. In addition, the sectors with the fastest transition to remote work in the research emerged as e-commerce, media, advertising, medicine, construction and technology. On the other hand, health personnel, security forces, those working in the agricultural sector, those who produce and distribute products necessary for the continuity of life, and those working in the retail sector have a very low rate of working from home. However, cultural characteristics and habits can also be determinant on the implementation and adoption of remote work. Working from home can vary from job to job as well as from city to city and from industry to industry. Gallacher and Hossain (2020) stated that 41 % of the jobs are carried out from home in Canada, and they stated that the rate of working from home is higher

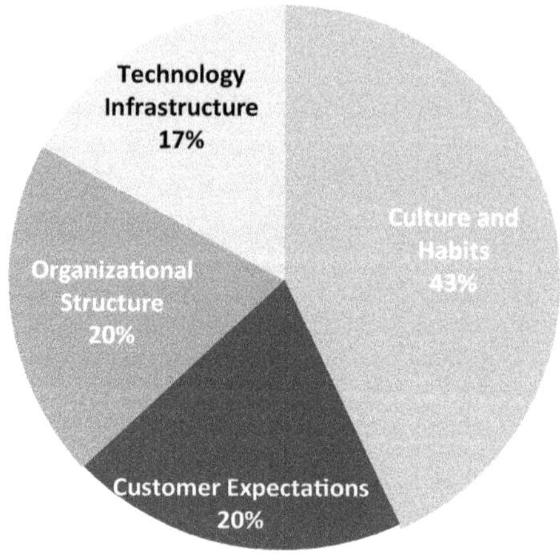

Fig. 1.3: Why are companies having difficulties in transitioning from home/distance work? (Deloitte 2020)

among high-wage earners, and women. On the other hand, it was emphasized that working from home opportunities are very limited and difficult for part-time employees, small business employees, seasonal employees, and employees without diplomas (Gallacher and Hossain, 2020: 45).

The results of Deloitte's research carried out with 334 participants from 17 different cities in Turkey on the difficulties in transition to the remote operation system in COVID-19 are shown in Fig. 1.3.

"Culture and Habits" (43 %), "Organizational Structure" (20 %), "Customer Expectations (20 %)" and "Technology Infrastructure" (17 %) are the most fundamental factors. Holdings are at the top of the sectors stating that "Culture and Habits" is the most difficult issue in the transition to remote working model, followed by the Energy sector with 66.7 %. This factor stands out especially in hierarchical organizational structures (Deloitte, 2020).

1.6 The Ethical Dimension of Teleworking

Ethical dimensions are very important in the home working system. While working from home is an alternative that many employees may prefer, many employees do not want to work from home in order not to be deprived of the advantages of the work environment. In this case, employers must make fair decisions about who works from home and who does not (Guthrie, 1997: 30). If there is a need for new staff, staff who agree to work from home should be hired. If there is no need for new staff and the existing staff do not want to work from home, these staff may be out of their jobs.

Working from home may result in employer's intervention in the private life of the employee. The reason of inefficiency of someone working from home may cause from problems in their home, and it is inevitable that the employer is also involved. For example, to determine the amount of home phone usage for business purposes, all invoice details of the employee can be seen by the employer. This is also a violation of privacy (Guthrie, 1997, 30).

In addition, unethical behaviors may be required when working from home, reaching the employee about the job, or reporting an urgent information. So much so that an employee who chooses to work at night and sleep during the day, or an employee who is sought out of working hours may be uncomfortable. These and similar situations may mean intervention in the private life of the employee. The existence of certain rules in the workplace environment in terms of work ethics, etc. practices provide respect for work, while working from home can eliminate respect for work. Thus, an employee's interest in working may be reduced if the employee's respect for his job is reduced.

1.7 Precautions to Be Taken and Recommendations to Employees

Recommendations for Managers and Leaders: Managers and leaders have the most important role in maintaining the remote working model successfully. Getting the balance right is one of the most important issues. At this point, it is of paramount importance, for example, to encourage employees to be free at the end of the working day and to maintain an appropriate work-life balance. Leaders should work remotely if necessary to understand employees and thus empathize with employees. They should motivate employees by focusing on the benefit of working remotely. By keeping communication strong, they should not leave them in the dark. They should also communicate with team members individually. In cases where things go wrong, they should provide feedback and help in finding solutions without wasting time. Feedback should be provided to the employee by measuring performance. Managers need to benefit from constantly developing collaboration tools and technologies and be a pioneer by following innovations.

Open Communication: Employees should be in frequent and open communication with their colleagues, managers, customers, suppliers and other stakeholders they cooperate with. They should ensure that they express themselves more accurately by determining daily and/or weekly information times.

Effective Working: Employees must identify the right workspace to focus on at home. They can increase their motivation and concentration by organizing this area like the working environment in their office. They should also plan their working hours and take care to act in a routine according to this plan.

Use of Technology: It is necessary to make maximum use of technology tools for cooperation. Frequent communication should be established through virtual meetings, video conferences, SMS and messaging applications, phone and e-mail. It is necessary to use visual communication tools more frequently, considering that words are 7 %, tone of voice 38 % and body language 55 % important in effective communication.

Being Accessible: Employees should share their contact information with their collaborators and make them feel accessible even when they are physically distant.

Leaders of remote teams have more responsibility to adopt a remote working culture. When working remotely, team leaders should ensure clarity of roles, responsibilities and goals and share them with the team. Team leaders should regularly schedule periodic meetings with their teams to discuss bottlenecks, what went well, and what could be further improved while working remotely in this working model. The team leader is responsible for resolving potential conflicts and misunderstandings between all team members effectively and in a timely manner.

1.8 Conclusion

Although teleworking has been used in several sectors for a long time, it has recently been used in many sectors. Working from home is an example of innovation, as Schumpeter points out in his creative destruction approach. According to this approach, innovations should continue to develop by removing the old and organizations should keep up with this development and change. While working from home can be applied effectively in some sectors, it cannot be applied in sectors that require direct contact with customers such as health, production, and transportation (Mustajab et al., 2020).

It will be easier for the employees to adopt the remote working culture if important factors such as how the work will be done from home, in what time periods and how the support of the organization will be determined. Mutual trust, leader's support, time management, performance measurement method supporting homeworkers, self-motivation ability, effective communication and disciplined work are the most important factors in the formation of this culture.

It is expected that the automation journey and changes in the way of doing business will increase employee productivity, and employees will focus on innovation, creativity and problem solving and equip themselves with different competencies. However, failure to provide a culture of working from home may lead to various discrimination and ethical problems among employees. Competencies mentioned here not only includes technical competencies but also some behavioral norms.

Employees working remotely must have certain competencies in order to have a high performance. In particular, they should have high internal motivation and self-ownership. They should not interrupt their communication by constantly informing their managers and their team about their work. They should get into the habit of helping people who need help. The most important factor in working remotely is trust. The employee should trust to his/her manager and friends and the manager must trust the employees. Because there is no one-to-one marking or close contact in the follow-up of the work, it is necessary to trust the person in front of you about the job. Promises and commitments made must be fulfilled in a timely manner. The homeworker should make a time plan and act according to this time schedule. At the same time, it should create a physical environment to work professionally. Working in front of the television, in the kitchen, or on a sofa in the living room will not be effective and efficient.

Considering all these conditions, working from home should be analyzed well and strategies should be developed in this regard. Employers may use the method of working from home to avoid some costs, but a poorly planned method can cause disruption to work and inefficiency of staff. Therefore, the conditions should be planned with technical analysis.

Employees must first recognize their own competencies. In particular, they need to know if they are psychologically suitable for working from home. At the same time, they must physically create their own working environment at home and comply with their working hours. Ultimately, the ways of working from home should be regulated legally by the states, and those who work at home should not suffer any loss of rights compared to those who work at work.

References

Acar, P., & Acar, A. Z. (2019). İşletmelerde Uzaktan Çalışanların Yönetilmesi: Lojistik Sektöründe Nitel Bir Alan Araştırması. *Ömer Halisdemir Üniversitesi İktisadi Ve İdari Bilimler Fakültesi Dergisi*, 12(4), 514–526.

Bailey, N. B. K. D. E., & Kurland, N. B. (1999). The Advantages and Challenges of Working Here, There, Anywhere, and Anytime. *Organizational Dynamics*, 28(2), 53–68.

Bentley, K., & Yoong, P. (2000). Knowledge Work and Telework: An Exploratory Study. *Electronic Networking Applications and Policy*, 10(4), 346–356.

Bouziri, H., Smith, D. R., Descatha, A., Dab, W., & Jean, K. (2020). Working from Home in the Time of COVID-19: How to Best Preserve Occupational Health? *Occupational and Environmental Medicine*, 77(7), 509–510.

Clark, S. C. (2000). Work-Family Border Theory: A New Theory of Work-Family Balance. *Human Relations*, 53(6), 747–770.

Deloitte (2020). https://www2.deloitte.com/content/dam/Deloitte/tr/Documents/human-capital/isin-gelecegi-uzaktan-calisma-sisteminde-organizasyonel-dayanikliligi-korumak.pdf

Dockery, M., & Bawa, S. (2020). Working From Home in the COVID-19 Lockdown. *Bankwest Curtin Economics Centre Research Brief COVID-19*, 1–5.

Fadinger, H., & Schymik, J. (2020). *The Effects of Working from Home on COVID-19 Infections and Production. A Macro Economic Analysis for Germany*. University of Bonn and University of Mannheim, Germany.

Gallacher, G., & Hossain, I. (2020). Remote Work and Employment Dynamics under COVID-19: Evidence from Canada. *Canadian Public Policy*, 1–24.

Gray, M. et al. (1995). *Teleworking Explained*. John Wiley & Sons.

Gupta, A. (2020). Accelerating Remote Work after COVID-19. *COVID Recovery Symposium*, 1–2.

Guthrie, R. (1997). The Ethics of Telework. *Information Systems Management*, 14(4), 29–32. DOI: 10.1080/10580539708907072.

Harrison, N. (2001). Teleworking from Home, (Çevrimiçi). http://www.ariadne.ac.uk/issue/17/teleworking/

Hobbs, D., & Armstrong, J. (1998). An Experimental Study of Social and Psychological Aspects of Teleworking. *Facilities*, 16(12–13), 366–371.

ILO (2020). Defining and Measuring Remote Work, Telework, Work at Home and Home-Based Work. *COVID-19: Guidance for Labour Statistics Data Collection*. Retrieved from https://www.ilo.org/wcmsp5/groups/public/---dgreports/---stat/documents/publication/wcms_747075.pdf, (18.09.2020)

Irawanto, D. W. (2020). Unexpected and Habit Driven: Perspectives of Working from Home during the COVID-19 Pandemic. *Asia Pacific Management and Business Application*, 8(3), 165–168.

Kaya, M., & Burtan Doğan, B. (2016). Esnek Çalışma Modeli: Ev Eksenli Çalışma. *Elektronik Sosyal Bilimler Dergisi*, 15(58), 1069–1099.

Koçak, O., & Kavi, E. (2010). Bilgi Toplumunda Evden Çalışmanın Etik Boyutu. *Sosyal Siyaset Konferansları Dergisi*, 59, 69–88.

Kreiner, G. E., Hollensbe, E. C., & Sheep, M. L. (2009). Balancing Borders and Bridges: Negotiating the Work-Home Interface via Boundary Work Tactics. *Academy of Management Journal*, 52, 704–730.

Lim, V. K. G., & Teo, T. S. H. (2000). To Work or Not to Work at Home: An Empirical Investigation of Factors Affecting Attitudes towards Teleworking. *Journal of Managerial Psychology*, 15(6), 560–586. https://doi.org/10.1108/02683940010373392.

Meltem, A, & Küçükoğlu, M. T. (2020). COVID-19 Ve İş Yaşamına Etkileri: Evden Çalışma. *Uluslararası Yönetim Eğitim Ve Ekonomik Perspektifler Dergisi*, 8(1), 71–81.

Mills, J. E., Ellison, C. W., Werner, W., & Clay, J. M. (2001). Employer Liability for Telecommuting Employees. *Cornell Hotel and Restaurant Administration Quarterly*, October–November, pp. 48–59.

Mustajab, D., Bauw, A., Rasyid, A., Irawan, A., Akbar, M. A., & Hamid, M. A. (2020). Working from Home Phenomenon as an Effort to Prevent COVID-19 Attacks and Its Impacts on Work Productivity. *The International Journal of Applied Business*, 4(1), 13–21.

Naswall, K., Hellgren, J., & Sverke, M. (2008). *The Individual in the Changing Working Life: Introduction* (pp. 1–16). Cambridge: Cambridge University Press. DOI:10.1017/CBO9780511490064.001.

Ozcan, O., & Ozturk, I. (2020). Impact of Organizational Culture and Leadership Styles on Employee Performance: A Research Study on the Banking Industry. *Research Journal of Business and Management (RJBM)*, 7(1), 45–55.

Pollert, A. (1988). The 'Flexible Firm': Fixation or Fact? *Work, Employment and Society*, 2(3), 281–316.

Rubin, O., Nikolaeva, A., Nello-Deakin, S., & Te Brömmelstroet, M. (2020). *What Can We Learn from the COVID-19 Pandemic about How People Experience Working from Home and Commuting*? (pp. 1–9). University of Amsterdam Press.

Srivastava, S.C., Chandra, S., & Shirish, A. (2015). Technostress Creators and Job Outcomes: Theorising the Moderating Influence of Personality Traits. *Information Systems Journal*, 25(4), 355–401.

Suh, A., & Lee, J. (2017). Understanding Teleworkers' Technostress and Its Influence on Job Satisfaction. *Internet Research*, 27(1), 140–159. https://doi.org/10.1108/intr-06-2015-0181.

Teo, T. S., Lim, V. K., & Wai, S. H. (1998). An Empirical Study of Attitudes towards Teleworking among Information Technology (IT) Personnel. *International Journal of Information Management*, 18(5), 329–343.

Topcuk, Y. (2006). Esnek Çalışma Ve Esnek Çalışmaların Sosyal Güvenliği', *Yayınlanmamış Yüksek Lisans Tezi, Dokuz Eylül Üniversitesi Sosyal Bilimler Enstitüsü, İzmir.*

Ward, N., & Shabha, G. (2001). Teleworking: *An Assessment of Socio-Psychological Factors, Facilities*, 19(1/2), 61–70.

Aybike Elif Bolcan

2. HUMAN RESOURCES MANAGEMENT IN THE DIGITAL AGE: CHANGES AND CHALLENGES

Abstract The Information Age, also known as the digital age, is the era when the development of information and communication technologies brought along social, economic and scientific change in human history and the network society gradually emerged. Technological developments not only radically changed our social and economic lives, but also significantly affected the management styles of institutions. One of the managerial functions affected by these developments is human resources management (HRM). The information age brings invisible rapid technological changes, and therefore it is a challenge for HRM to adequately deal with changes and work in an IT-focused environment. In this study, developments in e-human resources management (e-HRM) and its processes, which have been increasing rapidly in recent years, are discussed. The emerging positive and negative reflections to use these systems are also discussed.

Keywords: *digital age, digital employee, digital work, digital human resources management*

Technological development, spreading of information and communication infrastructure to wide geographies, and the fact that access to data and information became independent of time and place thanks to mobile technologies, enabled individuals, institutions and societies to carry out some of their relations with each other through communication and computer networks.

Changes in the technological field, the increase of international competition, developments in production techniques have accelerated the enterprises' attempts to make the best use of the existing human resources (Winarto, 2018: 33). In the information age, businesses are gradually integrating information technology (IT) into the management of human resources (HRM) to overcome technical challenges (Lin, 2011: 235).

The concept of "Human Resources Management," which was called "Personnel Management" until the 1980s, continued to develop in the form of "Strategic Human Resources Management" by adding an addition to its name in the late 1990s and early 2000s. In this transformation in human resources management (HRM), it is seen that a new term has recently been added: electronic human resources management (e-HRM). The "e" component is not only a symbol of technical progress but also a hallmark of the transformation of human resources (HR) within the company (Guiderdoni-Jourdain, 2009: 290–291).

Increasingly, information systems (IS) affect HRM activities in organizations. Consequently, e-HRM is gradually being adopted and introduced by many organizations.

2.1 New Concepts Regarding Work Life in the Digital Age

Our world is in a social and economic transformation led by communication technologies. This period, which we call the digital age, has brought along a new human identity, a new form of relationship and a new way of doing business (Platin, 2016: 103).

2.1.1 Digital Employees

Digitalization of employees was the first step that triggered this era. In fact, the people of this age belongs to a new generation called with various names such as Net Generation, Millennium Children, and Digital Natives. This generation, with their attitudes, characteristics, behaviors and expectations, met digital technologies at a very early age and live in a strong and permanent interaction. They can differentiate from the previous generation with thick lines with their ability to deal with multiple jobs at the same time, their flexibility in establishing relationships with others on digital platforms, their learning styles, their desire to be instantly appreciated and rewarded (Platin, 2006: 98).

Digital natives have digital dexterity, meaning they always have devices connected to the internet, and apps and web-based services are always part of their daily lives. Having these employees in the workplace, the organization needs to be digital in order to engage these employees (Sharon & Aggarwal, 2017: 24).

2.1.2 Digital Work Environment

Especially with the increase in the use of computers, the Internet and the intranet, both working conditions and ways of doing business in organizations have changed. In addition; mobile technology is an essential part of the IT revolution that incorporates technical communication infrastructure such as Wireless Application Protocol (WAP), Bluetooth, 3G and General Packet Radio Service (GPRS), mobile computing devices such as mobile phones and laptops, and can provide on-the-go computing support (Imperatori & De Marco, 2009: 36).

Information technologies have made it possible for individuals to work, communicate and collaborate anytime and anywhere. According to Parot (2009: 384), it is no longer necessary for individuals to be localized in the office, as they have all the useful information on their computers.

2.2 HRM in the Digital Age: Electronic HRM

The understanding of HRM and its applications in this field have also started to continue its effectiveness in a new field defined as e-HRM in a global competitive environment, under the influence of internet and communication technologies.

The concept of e-HRM was first used in the late 1990s, when the concept of e-commerce was widely spread. There are many different definitions of e-HRM in the literature: "a term that identifies a form of technology that enables HR professionals to integrate an organization's human resources strategies and processes in order to improve overall HR service delivery, the planning, implementation, and application of IT for both networking and supporting at least two individual or collective actors in their shared performing of HR activities" (Strohmeier, 2007: 18); "is a way of implementing HR strategies, policies, and practices in organizations through a conscious and directed support of and/or with the full use of web-technology-based channels" (Ruël, Bondarouk & Looise, 2004: 365); "conducting business transactions (and in particular HRM) using the internet along with other Technologies" (Panayotopoulou, Vakola & Galanaki, 2007: 278); "the composition of technology with the Human Resource Management functions and allowing it to be done remotely or digitally" (Siam & Alhaderi, 2019: 354). In summary, when HRM uses the internet or related developments and technology to assist its activities, frameworks, processes, it turns into an e-HRM at this point.

In the literature, together with the term e-HRM; it is seen that terms such as e-HR, virtual human resources (management), human resources intranet, web-based human resources, computer-based HRM systems and human resources portals are also used (Doğan, 2011: 53).

One of the main differences between traditional 'face-to-face' HRM and e-HRM is that in the traditional HRM, HR professional is the sender and employees the receivers of HR policies and practices whereas, in e-HRM, both managers and employees actively seek the information they need (Stein & Van De Muyzenberg, 2012: 256).

There is also another term close to but quite different from e-HRM: human resources information system (HRIS). "A human resource information system (HRIS) is an integrated computerized system used to acquire, store, manipulate, analyze, retrieve, and distribute pertinent information about an organization's human resources" (Kavanagh, Gueutal & Tannenbaum, 1990: 42). The fundamental difference between HRIS and e-HR is that HRIS is directed toward the HR department itself and end users mainly include the HR staff; while in e-HRM, end users are not the only HR staff but the employees and management (Zafar, 2013: 105).

2.3 Changes in HRM Processes

HR practices are of great importance in terms of both developing and internalizing organizational culture. In general, it ensures the selection of the employee, their placement in accordance with job descriptions, evaluation of their performance according to certain criteria, rewarding, continuing education and professional development activities, promotion operations, orientation of new members, reinforcement and continuity of the existing culture (Günsel & Pelenk, 2017: 59).

It is seen in e-HRM that most of the processes performed by human resources departments have been moved to the web. E-HRM can be used for many HR-related activities such as record keeping, recruitment, selection, training, compensation and performance management; and may be used to manage HR across the whole employee lifecycle (Parry, 2011: 1146).

2.3.1 E-Personal Affairs and E-Payrolling

Considered one of the most boring jobs in human resources departments, payroll and personal affairs are perhaps the most suitable functions for digitalization.

The creation of a personal file is defined in the labor laws of many countries and computer programs can be used because there is no statement about the way the files are stored in the laws.

The digitalization of the personnel affairs process begins at the recruitment stage. The job application form, transfer/assignment form, proposal form and personality inventory/competencies form filled in on the system are sent to the personnel department with the registration file opened on behalf of the person. The form containing the documents requested from the person whose recruitment process is started is sent via e-mail and verification can be made with barcode/QR codes while the prepared version is processed into the system. The declaration of employment is sent online to the social security institution. After the recruitment process, the role/title is defined on the system and the candidate is included in the hierarchical scheme. Thus, the manager who is the person who will approve in performance evaluations or in cases such as leave/advance approval is defined. In case of leaving the job; severance, notice, annual leave payment amounts are calculated, if the notice period will be used, the exit date is determined by the system and all the information collected (severance pay, notice pay, annual leave, missing days, benefits from benefits) are recorded on the payroll. The last working day exit documents (release, notification/waiver, last payroll, work document) are taken from the system and their wet/electronic signatures are taken from the person and recorded in the system. The social security institution dismissal declaration is notified on its website. Within the scope of the leaves used by the employees, annual leave, unpaid leave, rest leave, maternity leave, marriage leave, mandatory leaves (mine workers, x-ray workers, etc.) can be evaluated.

Institutions/organizations such as social security institutions, employment agencies and law enforcement offices, where their personal affairs are in direct contact, will make it possible to make online notifications possible in terms of catching up with the standards of the age (Şoray Erdağ, 2006a: 56–57).

2.3.2 E-Planning

Human resources planning process consists of information gathering and situation analysis, estimation of labor demand and supply and determination of human resources needs, development of action plans to meet human resources needs, and valuation-control stages. Computers and electronic media can be used at these stages

E-HRM systems provide tools that facilitate the collection, storage, updating of data about the existing knowledge, skills and abilities of employees in the organization, and accessing these data when necessary, and this enables faster and more informed decision making (Doğan, 2011: 53).

The judicial and quantitative methods used in determining the demand for labor can be made by computer. In judgmental methods such as manager forecasting, Delphi technique, scenario analysis, and benchmarking, computers can provide managers with a large pool of information to make more accurate decisions. Computers speed up operations in numerical methods that are more complex than judicial methods and require mathematical calculations. Numerical methods such as trend analysis, regression-correlation analysis, and ratio analysis are concluded in a very short time by using computer programs without the need for calculations with paper items. In this way, both time saving and mistakes in calculations to be made using pen and paper are prevented. Numerical calculations such as actual personnel requirement, reserve personnel requirement, additional personnel requirement and total workload required to determine these requirements, absenteeism analyzes, and workforce turnover rate are also performed more accurately and quickly through computers. In addition to these calculations, the possibility of storing the obtained information and data in electronic environment enables the changes according to years to be seen and comparisons to be made easily (Doğan, 2011: 54).

2.3.3 E-Recruitment and E-Selection

The process of selecting and evaluating human resources constitutes the most important issue that should be considered among human resources processes. "Recruitment process links employers and job seekers, thus it is very serious for organization to make the right choice and reduce costs for further search and selection" (Khlebadodava & Remeikiene, 2019: 25). Because the more accurately a company does the recruitment, the less labor it will spend and the investment amount it will make in HR processes such as management, training and development, and ensuring commitment (Arslan, 2006: 120)

Since the 1990s, businesses have been experiencing significant changes in their workforce recruitment processes with the development of information technologies. Before the intensive use of the Internet, businesses used traditional methods such as newspaper ads, employee references, and individual job applications in recruiting new workforce, today they have the opportunity to reach a wider market in terms of geography by using the internet-based e-workforce market and have the opportunity to make this process cheaper and faster than before (Güler, 2006: 20).

Corporate websites, online recruitment portals (cvonline.lt, kariyer.net, etc.), searching for the candidates over the Internet and social media platforms (facebook.com, twitter.com, linkedin.com, etc.) are the most popular ways of using e-recruitment.

Via corporate websites, businesses are able to post vacancies on the corporate website, and allow applicants to send their resumes electronically via e-mail or in some electronic format (Panayotopoulou, Vakola & Galanaki, 2007: 279). In addition, businesses can also perform applications such as recruitment and job postings on the corporate websites of the companies that professionally do this job. Since recruiting sites draw more applicants, many companies tend to benefit from these sites' candidate pools. Furthermore, less well-known and relatively smaller organizations can achieve better results using recruitment sites, as candidates do not visit their corporate web pages (Doğan, 2011: 56).

Although the usage rate seems low compared to other alternatives, the importance of social media channels is gradually increasing as they provide effective communication with the target audience to be reached. For example, PepsiCo has launched a contest simultaneously on Twitter, Vine and Instagram for the search for a Social Media Intern, and has given one person the opportunity to become a social media intern who has prepared the most creative application video or photo with one of their brands and shared them on social media (Arslan, 2006: 125). In addition, professional social networks are used to reach candidates, especially not actively seeking a job.

New technologies are not only useful in recruiting candidates for the organization, but can also be used in selection activities of these recruited candidates. "Traditional face-to-face interviews are still being used, but the range of assessment processes which inform the candidates regarding the selection is increasingly diverse, taking advantage of new methods and strategies, such as online personality and assessment testings and including in the process more of electronic-based tools" (Khlebadodava & Remeikiene, 2019: 25). For example, video conferencing and online testing were extensively used in the early stages of the selection process and can achieve spectacular cost and time savings (Panayotopoulou, Vakola & Galanaki, 2007: 290). "Online games" in which the player, that is, the job applicant, has to carry out a number of different tasks online are already used by various companies (Puck, Holtbrügge & Mohr, 2009: 188)

Artificial intelligence refers to a wide range of technologies that allow a machine to perform tasks that usually require human cognition, including making decisions and use of it in HRM, especially in recruitment, has been called the "new era of HR" in recent years (Johansson & Herranen, 2019: 6). In an application developed by HireVue, artificial intelligence is able to interpret and analyze the applicant's body language, facial expressions or tone of voice, comparing interviewed applicants with the most skilled employees in the company, and finally recommending the best applicants to recruiters (Johansson & Herranen, 2019: 7).

Providing access to more qualified candidates in national and international labor markets and therefore a wider candidate pool, making recruitment in a much shorter and less costly manner, shortening recruitment cycle times, being accessible 24 hours a day, integration with other computerized HR functions such as payroll and databases, providing a more efficient and paperless recruitment management, keeping digital records of video interview and online assessment center applications applied in recruitment interviews are the potential benefits of e-recruitment (Balmish, 2020: 29; Doğan, 2011: 58; Du Plessis et al., 2011: 6; Eronat, 2006: 115; Öksüz, 2011: 274).

On the other hand, with online resume creators and profile editors, it has been suggested that applicants' thinking ability and creativity is largely lost due to the fact that everything is easily available on the internet, that they only cut, copy and paste someone else's work, but do not mention their own qualities, and they sometimes deceive companies by making false claims (Du Plessis et al., 2007: 11). Also, some disadvantages may include interruption of face-to-face communication and discrimination against people without internet access (Balmish, 2020: 29).

E-recruitment will definitely continue to play a very prominent role as the world becomes more digitized (Rao, 2009: 227). Future generations who grow up with computers are unlikely to use conventional recruitment methods; they would possibly use e-recruitment only. According to a study conducted in 2013, "almost 100 per cent of job seekers under the age of twenty five would prefer the communication with employers online and not via phone and/or other sources" (Khlebadodava & Remeikiene, 2019: 27)

2.3.4 E-Training

Today, people's desire to access the information they want from wherever and whenever they want is an undeniable truth. As a reflection of this need, digitalization of training activities in businesses is a set of systems that enable employees to receive training without time constraints and independent of location, using various communication tools. Thanks to technological developments, it has become easier to evaluate education and training efficiency in electronic environment (Şoray Erdağ, 2006b: 33).

E-training covers all learning experiences that are sponsored by information and communication technologies (ICTs). New technologies can be used at every stage of training, starting with the analysis of training needs. Training planning can be done more rationally, thanks to the digitalization of all business data. After training; training evaluation results, training participation status, training satisfaction surveys are transferred to the digital platform and evaluated, especially through mobile devices, so that training effectiveness can be measured in a short time.

For sure, e-training has also some disadvantages. If workers are not positive and comfortable in using the technology, their performance would suffer in an e-learning environment. E-training might be isolating and reduce career enhancing network. "When training is conducted in a classroom, employees are able to engage with each other in the classroom and outside of it and these informal conversations and interactions can help employees broaden their personal networks" (Johnson & Gueuta, 2011: 15). Lastly, some training programs, especially which need practice, would not be suitable for e-training.

2.3.5 E-Performance Management

Performance management is all practices conducted by a company to enhance the performance of its workers, beginning with performance assessment and then feedback to the employee and ending with reward and training.

E-performance evaluation ensures that the entire process is carried out online. Managers and employees can provide performance assessment data to human resources departments via online forms. Self-service application allows managers to enter performance appraisal results and schedule employees' performance on their personal HR pages. These integrated systems assist managers to measure performance, assemble and write performance reviews, and provide detailed feedback to employees (Rondeau, 2018: 197).

These systems have the advantages of always being accessible from any computer with internet access, the ease and speed of generating HR-related reports, offering HR managers the opportunity to easily monitor the extent to which supervisors complete their employees' performance evaluations on time, and facilitate the review of trends in performance ratings (Payne et al., 2009: 528).

On the other hand, according to Rondeau (2018: 205), employee motivation can be potentially affected by the means by which feedback is provided, in other words, computerized feedback may result in lower levels of employee motivation loss when compared with feedback conveyed by a supervisor.

2.3.6 E-Remuneration

Wage is a powerful tool in motivating and rewarding employees. Organizations are increasingly using IT to support remuneration planning and management.

Generally; e-remuneration is used in the automation of the payroll system, the design of the remuneration system and its relationship with employee performance evaluation, and the management of wages and benefits (Rondeau, 2018: 202).

Electronic remuneration is the collection, storage, processing, analysis, use and distribution of data and information about wages on the web (networks). With the use of electronic systems, reports can be prepared and analyzed on the wage distributions or average wages by job, grade, age, length of service, wage differences between less senior and very senior employees can be calculated, future wage costs can be predicted, wage negotiations can be managed and interview forms can be prepared, and information to assist line managers in making wage decisions can be provided (Armstrong, 2006: 73). With electronic remuneration, managers can effectively design, manage and report fee schedules using web-based software tools. Employees can access wage software, databases and analytical resources electronically from anywhere – from their offices, their homes – by using the internet and web browsers (Doğan, 2011: 68).

Besides, benefits are an important component of every employee's wage. In electronic systems, employees use the web to convey information about their benefits, and they are given the opportunity to choose and manage their benefits online. Many organizations now make available outreach information through the HR portal, which provides details from health benefits to retirement contributions, leave information, vacation planning, and more (Johnson & Gueuta, 2011: 20).

One of the most critical aspects of any pay or compensation scheme is the perception of the system's fairness by the employees. Employees deserve to be equally paid for the importance of the job that they do, as well as with other employees in the organization (internal equality) and with other employees in the market (external equity). An electronic remuneration system, when well connected with a job evaluation system, can support employees' perceptions of both internal and external justice (Johnson & Gueuta, 2011: 21).

2.3.7 E-Career Management

Computer-based career management systems improve the consistency and amount of career-related services offered to their staff by organizations and is a screening tools that defines and describes goals for employee growth. Moreover, these programs provide an opportunity to compare employees' expertise and skills with the skills needed for their current and potential roles (Rothwell et al., 2005: 30). Human resources portals created in organizations also provides employees the opportunity to manage their own careers, get information about job opportunities within the organization, and benefit from training and development opportunities.

There are also websites that offer career counseling. These sites provide users with constantly updated detailed information in a convenient and accessible way whenever and wherever they want. Among the materials offered on the websites are tests, which evaluate users' interests, skills, abilities, business values and/or personality types. The purpose of this assessment is to collect as much information as possible about people's personal characteristics that affect their career choices (Doğan, 2011: 65).

2.4 Dark Sides of Digital HRM

E-HRM is important for all organizations in the digital age in which we live. However, transformation from conventional systems to modern IT-based systems has been challenging and this style of management needs careful research before adoption. Information security, cyber security, invasion of employee privacy, and ethical aspects of artificial intelligence are among the factors that should be considered and taken into account in the transformation process.

2.4.1 Information Security and Cyber Security in E-HRM Practices

Confidentiality, confidentiality and availability of data are very relevant for the businesses. In recent years, businesses have been facing serious challenges to information and network security that cause them to lose, modify and misuse their critical data (Çetin Karabat & Karabat, 2012: 46). With information security, it is aimed to be aware of the threats that may be encountered, to ensure the continuity of the work, to minimize the losses in all kinds of problems, and to protect the confidentiality, accessibility and integrity of the companies' assets under all conditions. An HR application contains data that should be well protected, such as demographic information, social security numbers, payroll data, performance history, and medical history.

Information security threats against companies are divided into two main groups: internal threats and external threats.

Cyberattacks, which are the biggest enemy of the digital age, have high costs for companies both in terms of money and time. A new malicious program emerges every two seconds on the Internet, and about a hundred new viruses appear every day (Böhme, 2015). Users around the world are exposed to intellectual property theft and identity theft, which focuses on confiscating users' personal information and then using it to obtain confidential information through highly dangerous software attacks such as viruses and Trojans (Majeeda, Shakirb & Khorsheedc, 2019: 415). Since HR employees have the right to access personal data belonging to employees, it enables them to change and/or misuse this data. Confidential information may be leaked intentionally by someone, such as a disgruntled employee, or accidentally by someone who is not properly trained in the use (Zafar, 2013: 106; Çetin Karabat & Karabat, 2012: 46).

Ensuring input data protection and confidentiality is an essential problem in which workers feel "secure" while using web-based HR tools. The following measures can be taken by companies regarding information confidentiality and security: possession of a Disaster Recovery Plan such as cluster or backup, authorization, obtaining SSL (secure sockets layer) Certificate, ensuring security and control with firewalls, having antivirus software, establishing a system room where the entire IT infrastructure will be hosted (Balmish, 2020: 35; Kirman, 2006: 28–29).

2.4.2 Invasion of Employee Privacy

Employee privacy is essential in HRM implications. In fact, respect for the private life of employees and its privacy are accepted in the laws of many countries. These legal restrictions need to be taken into account in the design and development of e-HRM and in establishing privacy policies in organizations. Employers should be aware of national and international privacy laws when designing and using e-HRM to collect, store, use and disseminate data about candidates and employees.

One of the most typical examples of interference with employee privacy is the use of social media accounts in recruitment, which has become widespread in recent years. Websites on the Internet and social media provide a lot of personal and lifestyle information about candidates and employees. As a result, employers start analyzing the websites of candidates or social media sites to obtain lifestyle details or knowledge about their personal experience that could have a negative effect on job results (Zafar & Stone, 2017: 62). It is also possible that HR professionals search for and use such information from social media about current and future employees unethically and at times unlawfully to weaken and harm their careers (Davison, Maraist & Bing, 2011: 157).

Another aspect of invasion of employee privacy is e-performance monitoring. Electronic performance monitoring (EPM) is one of the technical advancements that workers experience in today's workplace, and it provides managers with access to the computer terminals and telephones of their workers, enabling managers to determine, at any point in the day, the pace at which workers work, the degree of accuracy, log-in and log-off times and even the amount of time they need to work (Aiello & Kolb, 1995: 342).

2.4.3 Ethical Aspects of Artificial Intelligence

As mentioned before, artificial intelligence (AI) is increasingly used in E-HRM processes, especially in e-recruitment. However, one of the most important features that AI technology lacks is empathy and human interaction, or the opportunity to get to know a candidate personally in the process of selecting and recruiting them (Gür, Ayden & Yücel, 2019: 154).

One of the major problems of AI-based recruitment is unconscious discrimination. The danger is that algorithms will be racist/sexist because, as opposed to the ideal, their construction represents the reality of the work experience; systems may therefore introduce unconscious bias (Reilly, 2018: 8). "Actions using those algorithms risk reproducing the demographic diversity – or lack thereof – that exists in the historical data" (Johansson & Herranen, 2019: 17). For example; in 2014, Amazon Inc., set up a team to build a tool to review job applicant's resumes, that utilized natural language processing (NLP) and machine learning (ML) to find the top applicants that would fit the job profile; however, the algorithm picked women because fewer women were working in the past and because men had higher performance scores. This caused Amazon to rewrite the algorithms to be unbiased, but it was concluded that such an AI system could theoretically develop a ranking system that could discriminate candidates to some extent in the future (Kodiyan, 2019: 1).

Implications such as data protection, ethics, labor law, technology, viability and recruiting criteria of such a system must be carefully considered by each company before implementing such a system, and once implemented, regular inspections should be carried out to ensure that the AI system operates within appropriate operational boundaries (Johansson & Herranen, 2019: 17).

2.5 Conclusion

With the development of information and technology, it is seen that there are changes in the management understanding of enterprises. Businesses try to catch up with the dynamics of change anticipated by information and technology in order to reach new markets. In addition, the new generation, called digital natives, is gradually entering the job market and in the future all employees will be made up of them. The ability to attract, maintain, and grow them remains a major challenge for HR professionals and thus becomes a must using e-HR systems.

Today, it is seen that many businesses are working towards the application of e-HRM. There is no question that technology has made gathering, collating and distributing information, and communicating with employees, simpler and quicker. More significantly it has the ability to reduce the HR department's administrative burden.

While such applications provide new opportunities and facilities for businesses, their suitability in terms of information and technological equipment is also discussed. In addition, the success of enterprises in implementing these processes depends on the quality of the human resources inside and outside the enterprise. In determining the technological innovation suitable for the business, the human resources within the operating style and culture of the business are also at the forefront. Furthermore, from human resource activities that move from manual/traditional to electronic processes requires a clear understanding of how the adoption and implementation of e-HRM can work effectively. The constraints created by the "user experience," the concerns about the disclosure of the information that the employee has about the employees in the "personal information-secret" nature, the way of doing business isolates and even alienates the employees are the birth pangs of this change. Fear of shrinkage in the HRM unit is another factor that slows down the implementation of these practices.

Consequently, in order to adopt e-HRM system successfully, all aspects, in other words, people factors, technology factors and organizational factors should be considered. All those should be successfully engaged with the design, implementation, and use of e-HRM system.

References

Aiello, J.R. & Kolb, K.J. (1995). Electronic performance monitoring and social context: impact on productivity and stress. *Journal of Applied Psychology*, 80 (3), 339–353.

Armstrong, M. (2006). *A Handbook of Human Resource Management Practice* (10th ed.) London: Kogan Page.

Arslan, M. (2006). Dijital İşe Alım. *Dijital İK*. Retrieved from https://www.kariyer.net/ik-blog/wp-content/uploads/2016/01/dijitalik-e-book.pdf. 15.08.2020.

Balmish, J. (2020). Human resources management and technology. *Human Resources Management in Canada*, ed. Dessler G. & Chhinzer, N., Canada: Pearson Education, 49–78.

Böhme, H. (2015). Dijital devrimin düşmanı: siber saldırılar. *Deutche Welle Türkiye*. Retrieved from http://www.dw.com/tr

Çetin Karabat, B. & Karabat, Ç. (2012). Increasing awareness of insider information security threats in human resource department. *International Journal of Business and Management Studies*, 4(1), 45–54.

Davison, H.K., Maraist, C. & Bing, M.N. (2011). Friend or foe? The promise and pitfalls of using social networking sites for HR decisions. *Journal of Business and Psychology*, 26: 153–159. doi: 10.1007/s10869-011-9215-8.

Doğan, A. (2011). Elektronik insan kaynakları yönetimi ve fonksiyonları. *Journal of Internet Applications and Management*, 2 (2), 51–80. doi: 10.5505/iuyd.2011.22932.

Du Plessis, A., Nel, P.S., Marriott, J. & Mathew, A. (2007). The use of e-recruiting methods: are they in a vogue and effective? Some views. *Proceedings of the 21st Australia and New Zealand Academy of Management Conference (ANZAM)*, ed. Chapman, R. Sydney.

Eronat, Mehmet (2016). Dijital ortamda insan kaynakları için veri ve bilgi yönetimi. *Dijital İK*, Retrieved from https://www.kariyer.net/ik-blog/wp-content/uploads/2016/01/dijitalik-e-book.pdf, 15.08.2020.

Guiderdoni-Jourdain, K. (2009). The enrichment of the HR intranet linked to the regulation's processes between HR actors. *Handbook of Research on E-Transformation and Human Resources Management Technologies: Organizational Outcomes and Challenges*, ed. Tanya Bondarouk et al. Hershey-New York: IGI Global.

Güler, E. Ç. (2006). İşletmelerin e- insan kaynakları yönetimi ve e-işe alım süreçlerindeki gelişmeler. *Ege Akademik Bakış Dergisi*, 6 (1), 17–23.

Günsel, A. & Pelenk, S.E. (2017). Yenilikçi insan kaynakları yönetimi uygulamalarının yenilik odaklı bir kültür oluşturmadaki rolü. *Uluslararası Turizm, Ekonomi ve İşletme Bilimleri Dergisi*, 1(2), 57–68.

Gür, Y.E., Ayden, C. & Yücel A. (2019). Yapay zekâ alanındaki gelişmelerin insan kaynakları yönetimine etkisi. *Fırat Üniversitesi İİBF Uluslararası İktisadi ve İdari Bilimler Dergisi*, 3(2), 137–158.

Imperatori, B. & De Marco, M. (2009). E-work and labor processes transformation. *Handbook of Research on E-Transformation and Human Resources Management Technologies: Organizational Outcomes and Challenges*, ed. Bondarouk, T. et al. Hershey-New York: IGI Global.

Johansson, J. & Herranen, S. (2019). The application of artificial ıntelligence (AI) in human resource management: current state of AI and its impact on the traditional recruitment process. *Bachelor Thesis in Business Administration, Jönköping University, Jönköpıng International Business School*, Sweden.

Johnson, R.D. & Gueuta, H.G. (2011). *Transforming HR through Technology: The Use of E-HR and HRIS in Organizations*. USA: SHRM Foundation's Effective Practice Guidelines Series.

Kavanagh, M.J., Gueutal, H.G. & Tannenbaum, S.I. (1990). *Human Resource Information Systems: Development and Applications*. Boston, MA: PWS-KENT Publishing.

Khlebadodava, H. & Remeikiene, R. (2019). Opportunities of e-recruitment through social media platforms and its development in Lithuania. *Journal of Management*, 34(2), 25–41.

Kirman, A. (2016). İç kontrol sistemleri ve bilgi güvenliğinin sağlanması. *Dijital İK*, Retrieved from https://www.kariyer.net/ik-blog/wp-content/uploads/2016/01/dijitalik-e-book.pdf, 15.08.2020.

Kodiyan, A.A. (2019). An overview of ethical issues in using AI systems in hiring with a case study of Amazon's AI based hiring tool. Retrieved from https://www.researchgate.net/.

Lin, L.H. (2011). Electronic human resource management and organizational innovation: the roles of information technology and virtual organizational structure. *The International Journal of Human Resource Management*, 22(2), 235–257. doi: 10.1080/09585192.2011.540149.

Majeeda, Z.A., Shakirb, A.N. & Khorsheedc, M.B. (2019). Compatible information security system for electronic human resources management encryption. *International Journal of Innovation, Creativity and Change*, 8(3), 413–427.

Öksüz, B. (2011). E-işe alım sürecinde kurumsal web sitelerinin kullanımı ve konu üzerine bir araştırma. *ZKÜ Sosyal Bilimler Dergisi*, 7(14), 267–283.

Panayotopoulou, L., Vakola, M. & Galanaki, E. (2007). E-HR adoption and the role of HRM: evidence from Greece. *Personnel Review,* 36(2), 277–294.

Parot, I. (2009). Coordination of virtual teams: from trust to control. *Handbook of Research on E-Transformation and Human Resources Management Technologies: Organizational Outcomes and Challenges*, ed. Bondarouk, T. et al. Hershey-New York: IGI Global.

Parry, E. (2011). An examination of e-HRM as a means to increase the value of the HR function. *The International Journal of Human Resource Management*, 22(05), 1146–1162. doi: 10.1080/09585192.2011.556791.

Payne, S., Homer, M.T., Boswell, W.R., Schroeder, A.N. & Stine-Cheryne, K.J. (2009). Comparison of online and traditional performance appraisal systems. *Journal of Managerial Psychology*, 24(6), 526–544. doi: 10.1108/02683940910974116.

Platin, G. (2016). Dijitalleştirebildiklerimizden misiniz? *Dijital İK*. Retrieved from https://www.kariyer.net/ik-blog/wp-content/uploads/2016/01/dijitalik-e-book.pdf.

Puck, J.F., Holtbrügge, D. & Mohr, A.T. (2009). Applicant information and selection strategies in corporate web site recruiting: the role of national culture. *Handbook of Research on E-Transformation and Human Resources Management Technologies: Organizational Outcomes and Challenges*, ed. Bondarouk, T. et al. Hershey-New York: IGI Global.

Rao, P. (2009). The role of national culture on e-recruitment in India and Mexico. *Handbook of Research on E-Transformation and Human Resources*

Management Technologies: Organizational Outcomes and Challenges, ed. Bondarouk, T. et al. Hershey-New York: IGI Global.

Reilly, P. (2018). The impact of artificial intelligence on the HR function. *IES Perspectives on HR 2018*. Institute for Employment Studies. Retrieved from www.employment-studies.co.uk.

Rondeau, K.V. (2018). E-performance and reward management. *E-HRM: Digital Approaches, Directions and Applications*, ed. Thite, M. New York: Routledge.

Rothwell, W. J., Jackson, R. D., Knight, S. & Lindholm, J. (2005). *Career Planning and Succession Management: Developing Your Organization's Talent-for Today and Tomorrow*. USA: Greenwood.

Ruël, H., Bondarouk, T. & Looise, J.K. (2004). E-HRM: innovation or irritation. An explorative empirical study in five large companies on web-based HRM. *Management Revue*, 15(3), 364–380.

Sharon, S.D. & Aggarwal, V. (2017). Digital human resources management. *Gyan Management*, 11(2), 23–27.

Siam M.R.A. & Alhaderi S.M, (2019). The scope of e-HRM and its effectiveness. *Polısh Journal of Management Studies*, 19(2), 353–362.

Stein, B. & Van de Muyzenberg, M. (2012). Human resource management in the information age. *Public Administration in the Information Age: Revisited*, ed. L.Th. M. Snellen, et al. Netherlands: IOS.

Strohmeier, S. (2007). Research in e-HRM: review and implications. *Human Resource Management Review*, 17, 19–37.

Şoray Erdağ, B. (2006a). Bordro ve özlük işlerinin dijitalleştirilmesi. *Dijital İK*. Retrieved from https://www.kariyer.net/ik-blog/wp-content/uploads/2016/01/dijitalik-e-book.pdf.

Şoray Erdağ, B. (2006b). Eğitimin dijitalleştirilmesi. *Dijital İK*. Retrieved from https://www.kariyer.net/ik-blog/wp-content/uploads/2016/01/dijitalik-e-book.pdf.

Winarto, W. (2018). Electronic human resources management (e-HRM) adoption studies: past and future research. *DeReMa (Development Research of Management) Jurnal Manajement*, 13(1), 100–120.

Zafar, H. (2013). Human resource information systems: information security concerns for organizations. *Human Resources Management Review*, 23, 105–113.

Zafar, H. & Stone, D.L. (2017). HRIS privacy and security. *Human Resource Information Systems*, ed. Kavanagh, M. & Johnson, R.D. USA: Sage.

Mehtap Aras

3. PROBLEMS OF KNOWLEDGE MANAGEMENT: SEEING THE DARK SIDE!

Abstract Nowadays, everyone knows that knowledge is power. Beyond that, knowledge assets are regarded as the most important strategic resource in organizations. The knowledge management field is highly complex and multidisciplinary. It is a field that concerns many areas such as knowledge, management, technology, organizational behavior, engineering, and software. Technological developments have been the most effective factor in the creation, access, sharing and protection of knowledge. The development of new and superior technologies can be an advantage for knowledge-based businesses as well as disadvantageous situations. Digitalization is a necessary but difficult process for organizations. Our focus is on the problems of knowledge management in the digital world. The main research question of this study is what are the points digital organizations should pay attention to when managing knowledge and what is the dark side of knowledge management?

Keywords: *knowledge management, dark side, digital organizations, knowledge management problems*

Technological progress has become so rapid that it has become difficult for processes to adapt to it. All kinds of businesses (marketing, service, production, software, etc.) must adapt to digital technologies and digital change. The digitalization of an organization means using digital technologies in each unit of it. Snow et al. (2017: 2) indicate that digital technologies include "computer hardware, software, transmission networks, protocols, programming languages, very large-scale integrated circuits, algorithms, and all the components and practices that belong to these various technologies." Besides, mobile applications and social media.

The most important reason for the increasing interest of organizations in knowledge management is that it provides a competitive advantage to the business and increases business performance. To provide a competitive advantage, organizations should adapt to the digital age. Knowledge management has three dimensions: people (knowledge workers), processes and technology. Technological developments affect all these dimensions. Digitalization naturally affects employees, technology and therefore the entire system. They influence one another within a chain. In digitalized organizations, knowledge management is also affected by each and this causes some problems.

3.1 Knowledge

A question that "What is knowledge?" has been considering by philosophers for centuries. However, there is no consensus on the definition of knowledge, on the contrary, there are many different opinions. The concept of knowledge for businesses is different from the term which is the subject of epistemology. In our field definition of knowledge is "the foundation of all aspects of the businesses" (Wiig, 1993: 3).

Generally, "information" and "knowledge" terms are often used interchangeably, we can also add the term "data." Skyrme (1999: 47) defines data, information, and knowledge terms as follows: Data is defined as facts and figures. Information is data with context and knowledge is information with meaning. The word "knowledge" has more than one meaning in English. It means information, awareness, learning, knowing, experience, skill, insight, know-how, and so on (Sveiby, 1997: 29). According to Wiig (1993: 10), the best knowledge in organization must be made available and embedded in all products and services to maximize value to customers.

3.2 Definition of Knowledge Management

Why do organizations need knowledge management (KM)? That is because knowledge management covers all processes of knowledge and each one is very important. Every single process that is so important to the business needs to be managed. Knowledge management requires organizations to adapt to changing conditions and to increase their competitiveness against their competitors with the knowledge they have.

Knowledge management as a field is concerned with all these knowledge management processes. Knowledge management processes are creating, share, use, transfer, mobilize, store, organize, retrieve, and apply organizational know-how towards the attainment of business objectives (Anand and Singh, 2011; Davenport, 2005; Despres and Chauvel, 2000; Desouza, 2007; Fong and Choi, 2009; Holsapple and Joshi, 1999; Skyrme, 1999; Soliman and Spooner, 2000; Wiig, 1993; Zbuchea and Vidu, 2018).

Many authors have looked at the processes of knowledge within organizations from different perspectives. This is necessary given that knowledge management is unique in every organization. According to some authors, the phases of the knowledge management process are as follows:

- Wiig (1993: 18); creation, manifestations, use, transfer,
- Chen and Chen (2006: 19); creation, conversion, circulation, completion,
- Fong and Choi (2009: 122); acquisition, creation, storage, distribution, use, maintaining,
- Anand and Singh (2011: 935); capture and creation, organization and retention, dissemination, utilization.

One of the main purposes of knowledge management is to store the knowledge of the organization in various ways and providing the most common and shortest possible access to knowledge (Martensson, 2000: 209). The other purposes of knowledge management are supporting the creation of knowledge, fast decision making, saving time, ensuring coordination between knowledge workers, encourage knowledge sharing by providing transparency, reduction of risk, supporting innovation, managing knowledge as an asset.

When talking about knowledge management and deciding how to manage it, it is necessary to consider the intellectual capital, the knowledge-based business, and the intangible assets of the business (Quintas et al., 1997: 385). Intellectual capital is the intelligence and knowledge-based assets of the business (Özevren, 2008: 52) and maximizes the organization's potential to create value (Dalkir, 2011: 430).

3.3 Intellectual Capitals

Human capital	in the minds of individuals: knowledge, competencies, experience, know-how, etc.
Structural capital	the codified knowledge, culture, values, norms, processes, information systems, databases, etc.
Customer capital	customer relationships, brands, trademarks, etc.

Skyrme 1999, p. 58; Dalkir 2011, p. 430

Wasted time comprises about 60 % of total operational time in most businesses, that is, working with wrong data and reinvention of the existing knowledge. The reason for this is the lack of an effective knowledge management system (Ameri and Dutta, 2005: 582). Managing knowledge is as important as creating and protecting it. Businesses can design their own knowledge management systems. For knowledge management to be successful in all their processes, it must work effectively. Knowledge management systems provide organizations to manage knowledge efficiently. A poor knowledge management system can cause the entire knowledge-based system to collapse.

The factors that influence knowledge management processes are culture, leadership, knowledge technology, organizational adjustment, evaluation of knowledge management activities and/or knowledge resources, governing/administering knowledge activities and/or knowledge resources, the motivation of employees, and external factors (Holsapple and Joshi, 1999, 2000: 238–239).

3.4 Problems of Knowledge Management

Managing already contains several difficulties and problems due to its nature. While managing people is a difficult task, following technological developments, adapting them to the business, helping employees to learn, adapt to these technological developments, and developing knowledge protection strategies becomes even more difficult for managers in digital organizations. With digitalization, "managers become so-called digital managers who are expected to have skills related to the use of ICT (information and communication technology) and know how to apply digital management techniques in practice" (Gonciarski and Swiatkowski, 2018: 338).

A knowledge-based theory relocates managers relative to whole the organization. In conventional organization theory managers are designing, resourcing, and controlling the organization (Spender, 2000: 165). According to Hinings et al. (2018: 2), "digital transformation comes from the combined effects of a variety of digital technologies that bring about novel actors, processes, procedures, values, and beliefs that change, challenge, substitute, or complement existing game rules within organizations, ecosystems, industries, or fields." Thus, digitalization puts an additional burden on both businesses and managers.

Although they differ from each other, knowledge management also has problems as in all areas of management. Knowledge management is closely connected to data technology, organizational digitization, and technological innovations (Zbuchea and Vidu, 2018: 697). In the digital age, managers need to renew and improve themselves. In fact, management problems (developing a new leadership style, managing people in new organizational structures, learning information technologies, and following innovations) in digitalization start with administrative problems (Gonciarski and Swiatkowski, 2018: 339).

Dalkir (2011: 425) takes the following view: Although technology can support knowledge and knowledge management, knowledge management is not a technology-based concept. Knowledge management designs should be based on who/whom (people), what (knowledge), and why (business objectives). Businesses should save how (technology) for last. The focus of knowledge management should be human and the knowledge that she/he create, transfer, use, so on. According to Barachini (2009), KM is not just an IT (information technology) problem. It is primarily to discover how people can be inspired to share useful knowledge so that business intellectual capital can be leveraged.

Bryant (2006: 4) underlines this view: *Knowledge is a process, not an object, and that knowledge management is all about people, not technology.* Bryant (2006) also states that this idea is a situation that undermines and contradicts knowledge management. Barachini (2009) claim that "knowledge management is not only an IT (Information Technology) challenge." Knowledge management is about how to motivate employees to share valuable knowledge so that businesses can take advantage of their intellectual capital.

The question confuses: Should the focus of knowledge management be human or technology? The answer to this question is both. Digitalization and technology are almost synonymous with businesses. Taking only technology or people as the focal point of information management would be a faulty management style. Human is always the most important part of management. In the digital age, the most important element is technology. Knowledge management should adapt to manage both human and technology.

Alavi and Leidner (1999: 13) summarized perspectives on knowledge management:

Desouza (2007: 10–11) states that many of the organizations he consults do not show enough importance to protect knowledge and knowledge management system. He makes three important points on this issue: First, he states that they have very basic problems in knowledge management and that knowledge workers are not yet good enough even in sharing knowledge. Second, in organizations with better knowledge management systems, there is a feeling that putting in security measures might derail the spirit of knowledge sharing and openness, and third, organizations have a difficult time identifying what knowledge to protect. Besides that, the major problems encountered in knowledge management often arise from businesses ignoring people and culture (Dalkir, 2011: 424).

As can be seen, besides management problems, knowledge management also has its own specific and significant problems. The digitalization process and the need for digitalization are creating additional jobs and challenges for companies, and particularly their managers. When managing knowledge in a digitalizing organization, people or technology will be the priority? Management

Information-based KM	Technology-based KM	Culture-based KM
Actionable information	Data mining	Collective learning
Categorizing of data	Data warehouses	Continuous learning
Corporate yellow pages	Executive information systems	Intellectual property cultivation
Filtered information	Expert systems	Learning organization
Free text and concepts	Intelligent agents	
People information archive	Intranet	
Readily accessible information	Multimedia	
	Search engines	
	Smart systems	

Tab. 3.1: Perspectives on knowledge management

must solve all these problems because each of them affects the functioning of the entire system.

The problems faced by knowledge management in digitalizing organizations are as follows:

3.4.1 Adapting to Knowledge Technologies/Cost of Adapting New Technology

Digitalization makes it imperative to adapt technological developments to the business. Since the end of the 1980s, businesses have followed the technological developments and started to apply them rapidly. Their rapid adaptation of ICTs requires the development and adoption of appropriate tools, tactics, techniques, and technologies to facilitate the management of knowledge management assets (Wickramasinghe et al., 2009: 2–3). Organizations use ICT as a strategic tool for KM initiatives (Alavi et al., 2006: 193). Chandan (2013: 302) listed ICTs-based knowledge tools as follows: groupware systems, intranet and extranet document management systems, data warehousing, data mining, decision support systems. To restructure the knowledge management, it firstly needs software, communication, knowledge sharing, and workflow management (Hermann, 2011: 32).

Adapting to knowledge technology and technological solutions are costly (Hermann, 2011: 32). The costs of developing high-tech products or using high-tech products are too high, for example over $250 million spent on Microsoft Windows 95 (Teece, 2000: 46). Skyrme (1999: 197) points out that 80 % of the investments are spent on training, database maintenance and content creation, while the remainder is spent on hardware and software.

In the age of digitalization, this cost increases exponentially. Apart from the benefits of innovations to businesses, there are also various burdens on the business. Businesses want to adapt to each innovation to increase their performance and productivity. This harmony also brings workload to the employees. Learning is a time-consuming task. Time is important to every business employee, and even more to knowledge employees. To manage knowledge, it is necessary to adapt to technological developments. The biggest problems that managers face while adapting the business to new innovations are organizational re-structuring and its functioning.

3.4.2 Security Problems

Creating knowledge is difficult and takes time. Businesses that have the knowledge they can use after a long effort will naturally want to protect this information. They will try to ensure that competitors do not access or imitate this knowledge. Frishammar et al. (2015: 76) indicated that businesses can fall into a "weakened state" caused by knowledge leakage. They also explain "weakened state" like that: loss of competitive advantage and industry position when technological knowledge leaks.

Businesses to improve their performance depend on their ability to innovate and protect their intangible assets (Teece, 2000: 52). An organization's knowledge resources must be tightly protected. In knowledge management, managers should pay attention to legal and institutional arrangements that enable organizational knowledge to be pinned down, and objectified (Spender, 2000: 153).

Desouza (2007) defines intellectual assets as "the bedrock of the organization." Intellectual assets can be protected by law, like trademarks, patents, copyrights, trade secrets law, licenses. Also, organizations can put 'firewall' protections against hackers (Liebeskind, 1997: 631). Intellectual assets be protected from unauthorized sabotage (Desouza, 2007).

Trade secret law prohibits the employee from giving information, documents, and other codified information about the company to anyone or any organization outside the company (Liebeskind, 1997: 628). If the trade secret information was created by an employee and the trade secret is in the employee herself/himself, then the enterprise must show goodwill towards the employee or make a confidentiality agreement (Aras, 2018). Organizations are legally allowed to impose and enforce rules on their employers.

Security problems can lead to waste of time, money, and resources. Knowledge workers who create new knowledge may cause a loss of motivation because the knowledge they produce could not be protected.

3.4.3 Ethic Problems

Ethics is defined as an individual's personal beliefs about whether a behavior, action, o decision is right or wrong (Griffin, 2015: 43). Right and wrong are based on notions of morality or values (Land et al., 2007: 3). Although there are generally accepted rights and wrongs in public, people's right and wrong may be different from these values. Sometimes people may not accept the general code of ethics. Even if they live in the same society, family structures, lives, and even education can differentiate their perceptions of ethical behavior. Hence, the solutions of the human-centered problems – like ethic – are always complex. It is difficult to reconstruct ethical feelings or behavior in humans because it already exists within her or him.

Knowledge management problems, in other words, the dark side of knowledge management, are often caused by unethical behavior. Ethical problems have two sides: *employees* (knowledge workers) and *competitors.*

Employees (knowledge workers). The source of knowledge is human. Therefore, all human-centered problems are also valid for knowledge workers. On the other hand, knowledge is valuable if only one person has it, and it can lose its value when transferred to others. Based on the fact that knowledge is power, knowledge workers may avoid sharing knowledge by maintaining this power. When she/he shares her/ his own personal knowledge, she/he may think that he will lose value along with the knowledge. At this point, measures must be taken to ensure that knowledge is spread throughout the organization. In knowledge-based organizations, organizational climate should be built on sense of a trust.

Competitors. Getting intellectual property in the hands of competitors is always a risk (Jamieson and Loeng, 2003). Digitization may pose a risk to the company from competitors who act unethically. Land et al. (2007: 4) have analyzed the issue of ethics in knowledge management in three dimensions: socio-economic issues, technical issues, legalistic issues. The business can prevent unethical behavior of competitors by taking certain precautions. In this case, businesses should develop information protection strategies against competitors. These are intellectual property rights, patents, trade secrets, and copyrights.

3.4.4 Knowledge Workers Problems

Each employee and manager who contributes to the intellectual capital of the enterprise is called a knowledge worker. Even though the titles vary according to the structure of the business, basically the titles of the knowledge leadership and their roles are *chief knowledge officer* (CKO, senior management position), *knowledge analyst* (lower- to midlevel position), *knowledge engineer* (lower-level position), *knowledge manager/leader* (midlevel position), *knowledge steward* (low-level) (Bergeron, 2003: 43, 58).

The first of the two most important characteristics of knowledge is its cost. Because reaching information or producing information is time and manpower requires. Having valuable information is an uncertain process involving research and luck. Second, it is the embodiment in employees (in humans) and information products (such as plans, products, processes, and machines) (Liebeskind, 1997: 625; Nelson and Winter, 1982). Knowledge is of human origin, it is the most important resource owned by businesses, but it is not included in the business balance, although it represents 75 % of the business's assets (Türk, 2003).

About 70 % of workers in the developed world are estimated to work primarily with information and knowledge (Skyrme, 2000: 308). Knowledge work cannot be ignored as they increase the productivity and efficiency of economies (Davenport, 2005). Knowledge workers take part in working groups, teams and communities identified as the most important analysis and response unit in KM (Maier, 2007: 163).

- *Individual differences.* Knowledge workers differ from other workers in autonomy, motivations, cognitive abilities, aptitude for tasks, attitudes, and they usually tend to be unstructured (Bergeron, 2003; Davenport, 2005). Each type of knowledge worker needs to be managed differently (Desouza, 2007). This differentiation in the characteristics of the employees also affects the leadership style of the manager.
- *Leaving the organization.* If knowledge workers leave, they take intellectual assets with them (Bergeron, 2003). Confidentiality agreements should be made with knowledge workers. When split, there may be arrangements that will limit the work in the same sector for a certain period. However, confidentiality agreements cannot prevent employees from carrying the knowledge they have in their minds. The knowledge you create may one day turn into a weapon pointed against you.
- One of the problems of knowledge worker is *measuring their productivity and its cost.* Knowledge workers spend between 15 % and 35 % of their time

on information searches. These workers succeed in finding what they are looking for less than 50 % of the time. Knowledge workers spend more time recreating existing information. An organization with a thousand knowledge workers loses at least $6 million a year in the amount of time spent just searching for information. (Dalkir, 2011: 142–143). Unlike production staff, the manager is the owner of his/her expertise and his/her task is complex and imaginative and hence it is very difficult to control, monitor and manage it (Kovacevic and Durickovic, 2013: 95).

- *Commitment issues.* In knowledge-based businesses, knowledge workers are as important as the effective functioning of the knowledge management system. Businesses need a knowledge worker's commitment to keeping them. Commitment is both increases their motivation and decreases the probability of quitting. Businesses, as with other employees, should do everything necessary to increase the commitment of knowledge workers to the organization.
- From the point of view of the employees, the biggest obstacles to information sharing are the lack of a reward system that supports knowledge sharing, the managers' not supporting knowledge sharing sufficiently, namely the lack of motivation. Other reasons that prevent knowledge workers from sharing knowledge are that employees do not know who has the knowledge they need and do not have enough time to pass the knowledge onto others (Ujwary-Gil, 2011: 93). There is a need to create an organizational form and process that enables the flow and transfer of knowledge
- And also, the social networks affect the success and performance of the knowledge workers (Prusak and Weiss, 2007: 37).

3.4.5 Cultural Barriers to Knowledge Transfer and Share

Transferring and sharing knowledge is another problem. If knowledge resides in people's minds, data warehouses, files, or computer memories, it does not mean much for the organization (Goh, 2002: 24). There are several obstacles to knowledge workers not sharing knowledge. Knowledge transfer and knowledge management practices are influenced by the cultural dimensions (Alavi et al., 2006; Barachini, 2009; Bures, 2003; Mueller, 2012). Oliver and Kandadi (2006) use the term "knowledge culture" and explain "A way of organizational life that enables and motivates people to create, share and utilize knowledge for the benefit and enduring success of the organization," Janz and Prasarnphanich (2003) use "knowledge-centered culture" term.

Cultural barriers to knowledge transfer	Solutions
Intolerance of mistakes and need for help, lack of trust	Accept and reward creativity and collaboration, and ensure there is no loss of status for not knowing everything
Lack of time and meeting places	Seminars, e-meetings, redesign of physical workspaces
Status and rewards go to knowledge owners	Establish incentives, include in performance evaluations, develop role models
Lack of absortive capacity in recipients	Hire for openness, educate current workforce
Not-invented-here syndrome	Nonhierarchical approach based on quality of ideas and not status of source
Lack of common language (not just English vs. Spanish but engineer-speak vs. manager-speak)	Establish a knowledge taxonomy and knowledge dictionary for knowledge content, standard formats, translators, metadata, and knowledge support staff

Tab. 3.2: Cultural barriers and solutions

Oyemomi et al. (2019) research has shown that organizational culture has a very important effect on knowledge sharing. Organizational culture is an important element to promote the exchange, learning and creation of knowledge. One of the problems is how to convince, coerce, or directly get people within organizations to share knowledge that they have (Gupta et al., 2000). Cultural differences can affect value preferences regarding their knowledge and practices. Therefore, different knowledge management values can lead to different results (Alavi et al., 2006). Knowledge workers are more willing to share knowledge when they feel important by organization and when opportunities are offered for their personal development (Chandan, 2013).

Bures (2003) states that cultural dimensions that barrier to knowledge sharing can be divided into individual and social barriers. Individual barriers are "loss of power, fear from revelation, uncertainty, illusion of reward deprivation, single culture elements, difference between awareness and knowledge, conflict of motives." Social barriers are "language, conflict avoidance, bureaucracy and hierarchy, incoherent paradigms, underestimating of lower levels."

On the other hand, digitalization enables new bonds between employees with meeting software, instant messaging, video chats, project management software and mobile applications make it easier than ever before to stay connected (Gonciarski and Swiatkowski, 2018).

3.5 Conclusion

For the last twenty years, digitalization is not optional for businesses. No matter what field it operates in, it must keep up with the digital age in order not to lose its competitive power or to compete. Employees and managers may not always like change and transformation. Change brings uncertainty, and uncertainty is sometimes disturbing. Technological developments can disrupt an established organizational structure and functioning. Control and functioning are restored but takes time. Knowledge-based businesses may be more affected by the digitalization process. Although the problems that may be faced by knowledge management do not change much, digitization may cause new problems.

Digitalization, of course, provides many benefits to the business. Technological advances make many jobs and processes easier for businesses. For example, the contributions of the digital age to knowledge workers: accessing knowledge faster, creating new information easily, increasing and facilitating information sharing, faster communication with other knowledge workers. In addition to its benefits, it is a fact that digitalization causes some problems in businesses. This study focused on the problems that digitalization causes and can lead to in knowledge management.

To adapt to technological developments and the additional costs they bring to the business, the problems of information workers and the problems caused by information workers are problems caused by digitalization. In addition to these problems, security problems, ethical problems and the obstacles created by the culture in information management are the knowledge management problems of both digital businesses and all other businesses. As stated before, there cannot be a business that does not become digital today. All these problems are knowledge management problems of all businesses in the digital age.

We started the chapter with the idea that "knowledge is power," and we want to end by saying that "managing is more important than own it."

References

Alavi, M. & Leidner, D.E. (1999). Knowledge Management Systems: Issues, Challenges, and Benefits. *Communications of AIS*, 1 (7), 1–37.

Alavi, M., Kayworth, T.R. & Leidner, D. E. (2006). An Empirical Examination of the Influence of Organizational Culture on Knowledge Management Practices. *Journal of Management Information Systems*, 22 (3), 191–224.

Ameri, F. & Dutta, D. (2005). Product Lifecycle Management: Closing the Knowledge Loops. *Computer-Aided Design & Applications*, 2 (5), 577–590.

Anand, A., & Singh, M. D. (2011). Understanding knowledge management: A literature review. *International Journal of Engineering Science and Technology*, 3 (2), 926–939.

Aras, M. (2018). İşletmelerde Bilgi Koruma Stratejileri. *Ordu ÜniversitesiSosyal Bilimler Araştırmaları Dergisi*, 8(3), 613–621.

Barachini, F. (2009). Cultural and Social Issues for Knowledge Sharing. *Journal of Knowledge Management*, 13(1), 98–110.

Bergeron, B. (2003). *Essentials of Knowledge Management*. Hoboken, NJ: Wiley.

Bryant, A. (2006). *Knowledge Management – the Ethics of the Agora or the Mechanisms of the Market?* Proceedings of the 39th Hawaii International Conference on System Sciences.

Bures, V. (2003). Cultural Barriers in Knowledge Sharing. *E&M Economics and Management, Liberec*, 6, 57–62.

Chandan, H.C. (2013). Knowledge Management and Its Challenges in Global Business. In Christiansen, B., E. Turkina & Williams, N. (Eds.), *Cultural and Technological Influences on Global Business* (pp. 289–314). Hershey, PA: IGI Global.

Chen, M. Y., & Chen, A. P. (2006). Knowledge Management Performance Evaluation: A Decade Review from 1995 to 2004. *Journal of Information Sciences*, 32 (1), 15–36.

Dalkir, K. (2011). *Knowledge Management in Theory and Practice* (2nd ed.). Cambridge, MA: MIT Press.

Davenport, T.H. (2005). *Thinking for a Living: How to Get Better Performance and Results from Knowledge Workers*. Boston, MA: Harvard Business School Press.

Davenport, T.H. & Prusak, L. (1998). *Working Knowledge: How Organizations Manage What They Know*. Boston, MA: Harvard Business School Press.

Desouza, K.C. (2007). *Managing Knowledge Security: Strategies for Protecting Your Company's Intellectual Assets*. Cornwall: MPG Books.

Despres, C. & Chauvel, D. (2000). A Thematic Analysis of the Thinking in Knowledge Management. In Despres, C. & Chauvel, D. (Eds.), *Knowledge Horizons: The Present and the Promise of Knowledge Management* (pp. 55–86). Woburn, MA: Butterworth–Heinemann.

Fong, P. S. & Choi, S.K.Y. (2009). The Processes of Knowledge Management in Professional Services Firms in the Construction Industry: A Critical Assessment of Both Theory and Practice. *Journal of Knowledge Management*, 13 (2), 110–126.

Frishammar, J., Ericsson, K. & Patel, P.J. (2015). The Dark Side of Knowledge Transfer: Exploring Knowledge Leakage in Joint R&D Projects. *Technovation*, 41–42, 75–88.

Goh, S. (2002). Managing Effective Knowledge Transfer: An Integrative Framework and Some Practice Implications. *Journal of Knowledge Management*, 6 (1), 23–31.

Gonciarski, W. & Swiatkowski, M. (2018). Managerial Challenges in the Context of Digital Economy. In Brătianu, C., Zbuchea, A. & Viţelar, A. (Eds.), *Strategica: Challenging the Status Quo in Management and Economics, International Academic Conference* (6th ed., pp. 332–346). Bucharest, Romania: Tritonic Publishing House.

Griffin, R. W. (2015). *Fundamentals of Management* (8th ed.). Boston, MA: Cengage Learning.

Gupta, B., Iyer, L. & Aronson, J.E. (2000). Knowledge Management: Practices and Challenges. *Industrial Management & Data Systems*, 100 (1), 17–21.

Hermann, N. (2011). Barriers for an Efficient Management of Knowledge: Experiences from a Southern African Organisation. *Open Journal of Knowledge Management*, 3, 29–41.

Hinings, B., Gegenhuberb T. & Greenwooda, R. (2018). Digital Innovation and Transformation: An Institutional Perspective. *Information and Organization*, 28 (1), 52–61.

Holsapple, C.W. & Joshi, K.D. (1999). Description and Analysis of Existing Knowledge Management Frameworks. *Proceedings of the 32nd Hawaii International Conference on System Sciences*, Maui, HI.

Holsapple, C.W. & Joshi, K.D. (2000). An Investigation of Factors that Influence the Management of Knowledge in Organizations. *Journal of Strategic Information Systems*, 9, 235–261.

Jamieson, R. & Loeng, D. (2003). An Exploratory Study of Risks and Issues on Knowledge Management. *14th Australasian Conference on Information Systems*. Perth, Western Australia, 26–28 November 2003.

Janz, B.D. & Prasarnphanich, P. (2003). Understanding the Antecedents of Effective Knowledge Management: The Importance of a Knowledge-Centered Culture. *Decision Sciences*, 34 (2), 351–384.

Kovacevic, D. & Durickovic, T. (2013). Knowledge Management as Critical Issue for Successful Performance in Digital Environment. *Economics and Organization*, 10 (2), 89–99.

Land, F., Nolas, S.M. & Amjad, U. (2007). The Ethics of Knowledge Management. *International Journal of Knowledge Management*, 3 (1), 1–9.

Liebeskind, J.B. (1997). Keeping Organizational Secrets: Protective Institutional Mechanism and their Costs. *Industrial and Corporate Change*, 6 (3), 623–663.

Maier, R. (2007). *Knowledge Management Systems: Information and Communication Technologies for Knowledge Management* (3rd ed.). Berlin: Springer.

Martensson, M. (2000). A Critical Review of Knowledge Management as a Management Tool. *Journal of Knowledge Management*, 4 (3), 204–216.

Mueller, J. (2012). The Interactive Relationship of Corporate Culture and Knowledge Management: A Review. *Review of Managerial Science*, 6 (2), 183–201.

Nelson, R.R. & Winter, S.G. (1982). *An Evolutionary Theory of Economic Change*. Cambridge, MA: Harvard University Press.

Nonaka, I. (1994). A Dynamic Theory of Organizational Knowledge Creation. *Organization Science*, 5 (1), 14–37.

Oliver S. & Kandadi, K.R. (2006). How to Develop Knowledge Culture in Organizations? A Multiple Case Study of Large, Distributed Organizations. *Journal of Knowledge Management*, 10 (4), 6–24.

Oyemomi, O., Liu, S., Neaga, I., Chen, H. & F. Nakpodia (2019). How Cultural Impact on Knowledge Sharing Contributes to Organizational Performance: Using the fsQCA Approach. *Journal of Business Research*, 94, 313–319.

Özevren M. (2008). *İşletmelerde Değer Yönetimi*. İstanbul: Beta Basım A.Ş.

Prusak, L. & Weiss, L. (2007). Knowledge in Organizational Settings: How Organizations Generate, Disseminate, and Use Knowledge for Their Competitive Advantage. In Ichijo, K. & Nonaka, I. (Eds.) *Knowledge Creation and Management: New Challenges for Managers* (pp. 32–44). New York: Oxford University Press.

Quintas, P., Lefrere, P. & Jones, G. (1997). Knowledge Management: A Strategic Agenda. *Long Range Planning*, 30 (3), 385–391.

Skyrme, D. (1999). *Knowledge Networking: Creating the Collaborative Enterprise*. Boston, MA: Butterworth-Heinemann.

Skyrme, D. (2000). New Metrics: Does It All Add Up? In Despres, C. & Chauvel, D. (Eds.), *Knowledge Horizons: The Present and the Promise of Knowledge Management* (pp. 307–323). Woburn, MA: Butterworth–Heinemann.

Snow, C.C., Fjeldsta Ø. D. & Langer, A.M. (2017). Designing the Digital Organization. *Journal of Organization Design*, 6, 7.

Soliman, F. & Spooner, K. (2000). Strategies for Implementing Knowledge Management: Role of Human Resources Management. *Journal of Knowledge Management*, 4 (4), 337–345.

Spender, J.C. (2000). Managing Knowledge Systems. In Despres, C. & Chauvel, D. (Eds.), *Knowledge Horizons: The Present and the Promise of Knowledge Management* (pp. 149–167). Woburn, MA: Butterworth–Heinemann.

Sveiby, K.E. (1997). *The New Organizational Wealth: Managing & Measuring Knowledge-Based Assets*. San Francisco, CA: Berrett-Koehler.

Teece, D.J. (2000). Strategies for Managing Knowledge Assets: The Role of Firm Structure and Industrial Context. *Long Range Planning*, 33, 35–54.

Türk, M. (2003). *Küreşelleşme Sürecinde İşletmelerde Bilgi Yönetimi*. İstanbul: Türkmen Kitabevi.

Ujwary-Gil, A. (2011). The Analysis of Barriers to Knowledge Management. *Institute of Economics Polish Academy of Sciences*, 10, 84–102.

Wickramasinghe, N., Bali, R. K., Lehaney, B., Schaffer, J.L. & Gibbons, M.C. (2009). *Healthcare Knowledge Management Primer*. New York: Routledge.

Wiig, K. (1993). *Knowledge Management Foundations Thinking about Thinking – How People and Organizations Create, Represent, and Use Knowledge*. Arlington, TX: Schema Press.

Zbuchea, A. & Vidu, C.M. (2018). Knowledge Management in the Digital Era. In Brătianu, C., Zbuchea, A. & Vițelar, A. (Eds.), *Strategica: Challenging the Status Quo in Management and Economics, International Academic Conference* (pp. 696–704). Bucharest, Romania: Tritonic Publishing House.

Okan Yaşar

4. AGGRESSION STRATEGIES OF DIGITAL ORGANIZATIONS

Abstract Today in many business, the new quest is to be "digital." Companies substantially industries are devoting resources to become a digital company as a perceived tool to streamline business processes, place new products with additional technology, and reach more customers. As a result, digitalization has become dominant within the holistic strategies of organizations. While digitalization getting popular, the digital world offers not only bright sides but also dark sides for organizations. Firstly, digitization is no longer just an opportunity for organizations, but also a phenomenon of pressure. Old approaches and traditional strategies are already seen as unsustainable, but the big problem is how to strategize digitalization and how to digitize the organizational holistic strategy. Secondly, the digital world is turning organizations and industries into a destructive world. As digitalization transforms industries, it is vital for organizations to develop strategies to keep up with this transformation under time pressure. Thirdly, it is true that digitization increases efficiency. But this causes organizations to pay attention to the digitalization of only individual units, which leaves organizations only to efficiency-related issues, which is completely wrong. Finally, we can say that organizations pursuing digitalization have abandoned their strategies and have become having only IT strategies. These organizations trying to provide digital transformation mostly tried to organize business strategies and information technology strategies. This shows that organizations produce strategy at functional level. However, digital transformation and digital require a different adaptation set and different strategies.

The digital world requires organizations to move faster, and the digital practices of organizations that produce traditional strategies remain meaningless. Strategies and tactics produced by organizations in the digital world require them to continue their vision while increasing their decision-making speed. The recent differentiation created by organizations using digitalization has become a new topic of discussion in the organizational field. Digital developments have forced organizations to aggressively drive the way they compete, the way they interact with their stakeholders and their customers, and the way they create value. So the digital world makes it necessary to produce aggression strategy for new business models.In this context, this study aims, on the axis of the dark side of digitalization, to explore the phenomenon of digital strategy, to aware of basic terms on digital strategy, to discuss and to understand the meaning of digital disruption focusing on scope, scale and speed of the digital strategy to make a connection digital strategies with business models. Concluding, suggestions are made for the strategies of organizations exposed to the digital world, examples of the best practices and challenges for the organizations are discussed.

Keywords: *digitization, digitalization, digital strategy, dark side of digital strategy, strategy*

Organizations that successfully carry out the digitalization process and harmonize it with their strategies offer important new values for their stakeholders. Therefore, there is a significant increase in the number of organizations trying to adapt to digital strategies in both public and private sectors. However, a lack of information on digital strategies for organizations continues. The incompatibility of organizational strategies and digital strategies can be seen in the success numbers of digital transformations. Success rates in conversions have not exceeded 30 % for years. In a 2018 study, only 16 % of those who implemented a digital transformation strategy said they observed an increase in their performance. And 7 % of organizations observed unsustainable short-term increases. So this study aims to understand how organizations in the digital world align their existing strategies with digital strategies. For this purpose, the study covers a literature that goes from strategy general to digital strategy specific.

The most prominent examples on a global scale are Airbnb and Uber-type companies. These companies owe their exponential growth to their successful implementation of digital strategies. On the other hand, Amazon and Apple, using digital strategies as a competitive advantage by redefining their existing industries, offer great value to their customers (Bharadwaj, El Sawy, Pavlou, & Venkatraman, 2013, p. 473). These organizations have transformed not only themselves but also their sectors and disrupted existing business models. For example, while Uber disrupts taxi business models, perhaps, again with digitalization, autonomous vehicles will disrupt their model.

Digital capabilities and the level of technology owned are both opportunities and risks for organizations. Developments in this area facilitate the disruption of the environment and the way organizations compete in these areas. In addition, digitalization enables the organization to redefine its relations and behaviors with its stakeholders (Bharadwaj et al., 2013, p. 475; Pagani, 2013, p. 618). In this context, it is vital that organizations understand how to integrate digitalization into their current strategies, how to create and develop digital strategy. The representation of the digital staff at the C-level at the management level in recent years is one of the proofs of the increasing importance. Organizations have largely started filling the positions of Chief Digital Officer and continue to invest in digital solutions (McGee, 2013).

This study will enable us to understand the concept of digitalization and digital strategy, how digital strategy changes business models, and contribute to organizations' strategy in the digital world. It will contribute to the expansion of the literature in this field. It will also present how digital strategies differ from traditional strategies and provide a better understanding of the position of digital strategies. In addition to its contribution to the literature, it is considered that it will contribute to the understanding of more effective competition and digital strategy for practitioners in an increasing digitalization process.

This study includes three basic parts examining digital and strategy concepts. First part is to raise awareness of terms such as digitization, digitalization, digital transformation and digital strategy. In the second part, the scope, scale and speed of the digital strategy and the digital transformation process and its' challenges are discussed in depth. In the third part, the relationship between digital strategies and business models is discussed. The meaning of the concept of "digital disruption" is tried to be understood, how it destroys and changes not only business models but also the industry as a whole. Study concludes as some suggestions are made for the strategies of organizations exposed to the digital world.

4.1 Digitalization and Digital Strategy

There are a number of words related to digital as digitization, digitalization and digital transformation. In order to understand the concept of digital and its relationship with organizations and strategy, it is necessary to understand definitions first, and relationships and dimensions of each term lately. Digitization, digitalization and digital transformation are mostly used in the literature and also it seems there is a hierarchy between these terms.

4.1.1 Digitization and Digitalization

A distinction needs to be made as "digitization" and "digitalization" are terms that are often confused with each other. Digitization is the conversion of analog data, whose image is sound and text, into digital form, and the transition from analog to digital (Oxford English Dictionary [OED], 2014). Digitization explains the conversion of information from analog to digital form as a technical process (Negroponte, 1995), and sometimes it is used to take analog information and encode it as zero and one, as a result, computers can store, process and share this information. Taken as a process, digitization goes to transforming hard copy notes into an Excel spreadsheet. In this respect, digitization ensures that errors are reduced and productivity in operation processes increases. For example, someone who handles orders and shares them on paper consider the conveniences of doing this process digitally.

Digitalization, on the other hand, means the adoption and use of digital technology by the organization. Its use as a term has also been identified with computerization, and the digitalization process has been discussed in many areas including society. Digitalization is the process of transitioning to a digital business using digital technologies to design business model processes and create new value (Gartner glossary). When the effect of digitization on social structure is considered in the context of economy, society and culture, it is seen that the main determining factor is digitalization (Castells, 2010). The most important feature that determines social networks and society dynamics is again digitalization (Van Dijk, 2005, p. 156).

4.1.2 Digital Transformation

Digital transformation is also referred to as digitalization although there are some basic distinct. In the literature, digital transformation is defined as social phenomenon (Stolterman et al., 2004, pp. 54–58) or cultural change (Pardo & Etay, 2014, p. 133) and the design of business processes for organizations (Rothmann & Koch, 2014, p. 67). In terms of social structure, digital is perceived as a fundamental transition of the "digital" society in which the technologies used by the generation generations deeply rooted in society. From this point of view, digital transformation is a process that organizations have to adapt to change their business models. It should not be forgotten that this transformation will affect the organization in a holistic structure. The main areas of the organization which are mostly affected are their capabilities, models and processes. While digitalization is defined as an operational imperative, digital transformation is a redefinition of a business or even a sector.

From the discussions above, digital transformation is defined as the changes in the way of doing business due to the organization's use of digital technology. The organizational levels where these changes take place are process level, organization level and business level. Bringing new digital tools to the organization and speeding up processes by multiplying digital processes are related with p*rocess level,* renovating old processes, getting rid of old applications are take place o*rganization level,* changing ecosystem roles occurs on *business level.*

4.2 Digital Strategy

The strategy is made on the basis of some basic features (Hax, 1990, p. 35): Strategy enables organizations to determine the necessary decisions and priorities in order to achieve the vision, mission, goals and resources (Hax & Majluf, 1988, p. 101). The strategy is developed for conscious and specific purposes and implemented before actions. This situation is called the "intended strategy," the implementation of strategies against environmental changes is called the "emerging strategy" (Mintzberg, 1978, p. 935). Briefly, strategies can emerge in response to an evolving environmental situation or they can be formulated deliberately (Mintzberg, 1987, p. 68). It is not possible for organizational strategies to remain insensitive to the digitalization of the environment.

Digital strategies are expected to be compatible with other strategies, as there is more than one strategy development area within the organization scope. A digital strategy is one created using digital resources (Bharadwaj et al., 2013, p. 474). From digital strategies, it is expected that digital resources will be used in various functional areas of the organization such as supply, logistics, operations and marketing. Digital strategy will be defined not only with performance expectations of classical information technology but also with outputs that create value beyond the information technology (IT) (Bharadwaj et al., 2013, p. 475). The digital business strategy is formed by the degree of intersection of the organization's information technology activities and the level of interaction between the digital stance and the environment (Mithas et al., 2013, p. 513).

Since digitization changes the internal and external processes of organizations, their communication with their stakeholders, and the way they do business, it primarily affects their strategies. There are different studies in the literature regarding the achievements of digital strategy for organizations. How the competition formed in the external environment of the organization shapes the digital strategy of the organization (Mithas et al., 2013, p. 518), which values can be produced at which points in the networks formed by technology (Pagani, 2013, p. 620) were examined. Also; The scope, speed and scale of the sources of digital strategies (Bharadwaj et al., 2013), the need for change in organizations due to changing and expanding customer preferences (Keen & Williams, 2013), making digital adaptations outside of the organization, this can be copied by competitors and the competitive advantage may be lost (Grover & Kohli, 2013, p. 657) are among the subjects of this field.

4.2.1 Scope of Digital Strategy

Digital business strategy is organizational strategies in which digital resources are used and implemented, and are also formulated to create distinct value. In this respect digital strategy requires:

- To go beyond the traditional perspective, to use digital resources in the organization's supply chain, marketing, purchasing and operations,
- The spread of digital resources, the resource dependency approach should be included in the digitalization process,
- Linking digital strategies to the business value of the organization in a way that provides competitive advantage.

One of the main problems of strategic management is related to the activities carried out within the organization's business portfolio, namely its corporate scope. It has been demonstrated that the scope framework and the diversification approach of the organization are related to performance, core competencies and assets (Amit & Schoemaker 1993, p. 35; Berger & Ofek 1995, p. 47; Wade & Hulland 2004, p. 109). Understanding the limitations and scope of digital strategy helps to understand how the organization will interact with its external environment, IT, industry. At the same time, we can infer how the business scope is affected by digital technologies in which environments. Digital strategy differs from traditional business areas such as marketing, purchasing, and logistics. All functions and processes are carried out under digital umbrella, called transformational, based on detailed knowledge exchange with the internal and external ties of the organization. As organizations complete their digitalization transformations, they will become more confident in communication, network and information exchange, and digital business strategies will transform into the corporate business strategy of the organization. Over time, digital business strategy will replace business strategy as firms and industries become more digital and rely on information, communication and connectivity functionality.

Amazon business strategy can be a good example in this regard. While it is present in the online retail field, the fact that it provides web services on the cloud at the same time. Because it sees the cloud computing service as the main digital resource. These two areas can actually be seen as unrelated portfolio. A similar approach is seen in Google, Netflix, and Microsoft companies trying to benefit from the developments in digitizing their corporate scopes. Honeywell's next generation thermostats with internet connectivity, General Electric's healthcare solutions, Nike's digitized product developed with Apple, and others include the same point of view. It is the indiscriminate application of IT business strategy and digital business strategies that Apple and Amazon define their ecosystems in their sales processes. The main issues that underlie and need to transform are the agile redefinition of business processes in the digital environment, capturing interaction with the changing ecosystem, the transition from traditional tightly connected supply chains to loosely connected ecosystems.

4.2.2 Scale of Digital Business Strategy

The scales of business strategies in the digital field also differ in some respects. Since scale is the primary driver of profitability in the industrial age, it is necessary to think beyond physical factors and geographic boundaries, compatible with the organization's digital infrastructure. As products and services become digital, the effects of networks become more prominent in creating value. Digital network applications are expanding, as can be seen in the connections of Apple iOS and Google Android devices, as well as Open Graph and Facebook connections on the demanding side (Evans et al., 2008). Digitalization also describes business as a network structure connected with information and data. In this structure called the Internet of Things (IoT) (OED, 2012), there is a digital human and data network connected to each other. Re-development of organizational capabilities becomes important within constantly growing heterogeneous data networks.

4.2.3 Speed of Digital Business Strategy

While time is an important competitive advantage in strategic management, it has become even more important in the digital business world, which can also be called speed. Organizations that are at the peak of digitalization with Google, Facebook and Amazon are gaining momentum in developing and launching their products by taking advantage of the power in both hardware and software networks. While in traditional strategies the timing and speed of product launch can be determined by a single organization, it now needs to be coordinated with the partners in the product network. For example, Amazon's launching the Kindle is no longer a process it can control alone. It also forces it to be coordinated with both the android operating system and ebooks.

Technology does not only provide the advantage of first move by the speed it provides, but also offers opportunities for rapid movement in the global market. Thanks to ERP software, especially Oracle and SAP, productivity increase has been observed in almost every field. The integration of outsourcing outside core competence activities into a network has enabled the optimization of the supply chain (Klein & Rai, 2009, p. 740). The best example is Apple's inventory turnarounds twice as fast than traditional electronics companies and the industry average. Industry and societies are taking advantage of the speed of networking (Easley & Kleinberg, 2010). The digital business strategy designs networks that bring complementary capabilities in addition to the capabilities they have within the current hierarchical structure, and manages them in an institutional manner.

4.2.4 Sample Digital Products

Digitalization has become applicable in the products of every sector. From digital thermoses, lawn mowers, vacuum cleaner robots to soccer balls, they all went digital.

Adidas' soccer ball can collect data about shot power, ball speed, rotation and trajectory thanks to the sensor and can provide feedback with the application. This application, which helps to monitor the technical skills development of the players, also allows users to record statistics and share them on social media. Nike can likewise collect some data with running shoes and sync with the web. Users receive feedback on their progress and can share it with anyone and network they want (Arons, Driest, & Weed, 2014, p. 55). In addition, Nike collects marketing-related data such as when users run, what music they listen to while running, how often they run (Westerman et al., 2014).

While the digitalization of products seems to be an important step in the short term, in order for organizations to gain competitive advantage, it is necessary to use data to create value by connecting the analog and digital world. In summary, digital products will become meaningful as long as they create value, otherwise they will be products reduced to hardware prices if they cannot build new business models. Therefore, it is crucial to collect data that will allow digitalization to differentiate products and redesign experiences.

The next step of digitalization will be self-automation in decisions and processes. The dominant developments driving this field are Industry 4.0, artificial intelligence, IoT algorithms and big data applications. Strategy experts predict that these developments will lead to 30 % improvement in efficiency and speed (BCG, 2015). For example, Domino's pizza sees itself as a digital company and improves its processes digitally (Buvat, Kvj, & Sumit, 2017). Approximately half of the headquarters employees work in digital and data analytics, as a result, 60 % of sales are made in digital environments. It creates its stakeholders through digital ties. They provide their customers with voice commands and one-touch ordering with the platforms they have developed with Google Home, Ford cars, Amazon echo, smart watches. Customers can track when their pizza is cooked and when it will be delivered to them. Automating delivery and pricing with drones are steps currently being worked on.

4.2.5 Digital Transformation Strategy

The strategic plan is the process of deciding on the allocation of resources required to achieve goals. The main point here is to prioritize the contents of the digital transformation strategy. There are digital transformation strategies that apply to all organizations, whether private or public, such as technology use, value creation, structural change, financial features.

The technology owned and used is the indicator of the strategic effort of the organization. The organization needs to decide whether it *creates its own technology*, whether it *sees technology as the primary tool in its business processes*. Being a technology leader in the market, at least not being dependent on others in this regard, creates a competitive advantage. The business perspective is closely related to value creation. It is about which side of core activities of organizations are closer to on the analog/digital axis. Digitalization can be in products and services, enable exploration of new markets and new customer segments, and provide new forms of revenue growth. Using different technologies and creating different values with these technologies may require structural changes for the organization. What is meant by structural changes is that the owned digital products and services are placed in the corporate structure. The scope of digitalization determines the size of the unit that will drive the structural transformation. The financial structure can have a coercive and facilitating effect on the transformation process. Without waiting for the financial structure to force, organizations must face the need for transformation (Matt, Hess, & Benlian, 2015, p. 340).

4.3 The Challenges Ahead

Digitalization has caused changes in individual, organization and market behavior. While consumer behavior is mostly internet-based, mobile technologies, big data and the IoT have increased the performance of organizations. The pace of change in the market has increased even more with disruptive actors submitting new offers. As organizations try to keep up with this change, they seek to provide customers with personalized experiences.

According to a KPMG (2015) study on digital disruption issues, 84 % of French business executives are concerned about customer loyalty, while 91 % worry that a new entry will disrupt their business model. The digital transformation is more complex than IT-enabled and is one of the biggest challenges in all industries (Schuchmann & Seufert, 2015, p. 32). Organizations struggle to initiate and capitalize on this transformation and gain business advantage (Kane et al., 2015, p. 3). Studies reveal that minority companies have the right technological skills and develop the right managerial processes (Fitzgerald et al., 2014).

As the main obstacles to transformation and to have the right technology; there are lack of vision and inertia as leadership difficulties, attitude of old staff as institutional difficulties, aging technology and institutional policies. The fact that these situations are taken lightly and ignored by companies causes the problem to grow (Von Leipzig et al., 2017, p. 520). Digital transformation affects organizations from three perspectives by using technology; externally, internally and as a holistic. It presents customer experience and product life cycle in a digital context, changes digitalization of organizational structure, decision-making and business processes (Hess et al. 2016, p. 125; Schuchmann & Seufert 2015, p. 33).

4.3.1 Digital Disruption of Industries and the Re-shaping of Business Models

The way organizations create and present values reveals the business model of that organization and also gives clues about the business logic (Osterwalder & Pigneur, 2010). There are areas where digitization changes business models and processes, the main of which are: The substitution of labor in physical production processes; production robots, flood-check out systems, IP-based communication operators, digital sensors and watchers, self driving cars. New business models in the public as well as the private sector cause the destruction of unchanged organizations, and governments adopt more open data sharing policy to their citizens. The following paragraphs show how digital disrupt and re-shape business models and force organizations to change.

Changing hands of knowledge-based business processes: Reducing the need for field experts as the work of knowledge-based employees becomes done by data scientists and algorithms (Tsoukas & Vladimirou, 2001). In the near future, it is predicted that some of the decision tasks will be transferred to machines that have better information processing capacity than the human brain (Kurzweil, 2012).

Mass amateurization (Shirky, 2008). Reductions in transaction costs allow organizations to integrate many activities while reducing organizational hierarchy (Coase, 1937, p. 187). Mass amateurization, for example, turns into less professional work, as journalists turn into bloggers. Technology is forcing vertical organizational structures to change rapidly in recent years. Ronald Coase states in his book "Nature of the Firm" that vertically integrated companies are established due to the high transaction costs in the business world. Technological developments, especially the widespread use of the internet, facilitated transactions between employees, suppliers and customers. This development has enabled companies to focus on their own skills as well as increasing outsourcing (Powell & Dent-Micallef, 1997, p. 377).

Although all organizations were affected by these developments, some industrial areas were more affected than others. In some areas, there has been a transition from the physical world to the virtual world without having a physical structure (Peppard & Breu, 2003). Technology has also accelerated both the speed and impact of the destruction. The most well-known examples are Google's removal of the industry's giants TomTom and Garmin from the market within a year with the mobile map application, the rise of Alibaba in seven months, and Airbnb's more room reservations from Hilton within six months. Technology is providing organizations with new research and changing job descriptions of industries and breaking boundaries with other industries. Nowadays, Amazon's transformation adventure evolves into delivery by drone.

From Marketplace to Marketspace

Digitalization and internet are shifting business from the physical world to the virtual market. The main features of this new environment are (Mocker & Teubner, 2005). The following operations performed in the so-called online structure are not possible in the physical world.

- Quickly reaching end users and customers, enabling direct business and being widely used (Reich & Benbasat, 2000),
- Providing customers with a rich product range, facilitating information exchange with customers and providing appropriate answers to their requests,
- Interactive realization of public and business sector activities, realization of human-machine and machine-to-machine communication,
- Easy data collection, negotiations and collaborations, increasing the ability to solve collaborative problems.

Decomposition of the Digital and Physical World

Product development and review processes are shifting to virtual processes. Examination of physical objects by breaking them into pieces can now be carried out in virtual environments, inspection and data collection processes and maintenance decisions are also made in virtual environments based on these data (Jarzabkowski, Balogun, & Seidl, 2007, pp. 8–11).

Move from Push to Pull Economy

The digital world has led to the deepening of two different strategies such as push and pull in strategies. Although it is widely used in the supply chain and logistics area, it has become an overall strategy. The push strategy is summarized as attracting the product to the customer, while the pull strategy is summarized as attracting the customer to the product. Now attracting marketing, which has gained importance with digitalization, uses the internet and digital memories, especially media channels, to attract the attention of customers to a product or company and encourages customers to search for the product or company themselves. This method benefits from singular social behaviors by creating a viral effect. This is the reason why it has become popular in internet marketing.

4.3.2 Digitization and Data Restructuring Business Models

The business model is about how value is created and presented by the organization, and it constitutes the self-business logic of organizations (Osterwalder & Pigneur, 2010, p. 14). When considered in conjunction with big data, digitization challenges traditional business models. It is observed that traditional firms have difficulties in seizing and adapting opportunities (Weill & Woerner, 2015, p. 30; Westerman et al., 2014). Information management strategies discuss the literature, how digitalization reshapes organizational structures, division of labor, and business structures (Gable, 2010, p. 7; Malone, Laubacher, & Johns 2011, p. 7; Tams et al., 2014, p. 287). It focuses on how technology flexes these concepts, such as local changes in business processes, changes in working hours. This effect occurs not only within the organization but also in the inter-organizational sphere as integration with freelancers outside the organization and facilitation of cooperation with them. This structure works beyond the traditional outsourcing and institutionalized contracting system (Majchrzak & Malhotra, 2013, p. 258).

4.3.3 Deciding on Digital Strategy or Not

The size of the data the organization has and the rate of change of its environment will determine how much that organization needs a digital strategy. According to three possible situations, the course of action can be as follows.

- *Firms in the first group are those that usually don't have much business data.* If the processes of the organization do not use big data and this data is not related to the value chain, then that organization does not need to change its strategy. Typically, a company with a few specific suppliers and permanent customers is recommended to use traditional strategies.
- *The second group consists of companies that need certain aspects of digital strategy.* For companies in this group, digitalization and the use of big data are important for competitiveness, but not as important as their basic strategy. The areas where digitalization will be used can be the choice of

consumer behavior and sentiment analysis and the communication network to be established with customers. Coca cola can be given as an example to companies in this group. Digital networks can be utilized from marketing products to communicating with customers, but customers' experiences take place in physical environments at the end of the day.

- *In the third group, digitization has to become the DNA of organizations.* If big data has become a part of all business processes of organizations such as value chain, communication, etc., the organization cannot be expected to survive without digitization. AXA can be a good example for this group. The organization's business processes are completely changing, including the solutions it offers to customers, the data it collects from customers, and the way employees work. As a result, AXA's corporate strategy and structure has to change. The pay-as-you-go system it developed changes both the car insurance process and the rental processes.

4.3.4 How to Tackle Digital Disruption

As digitalization transforms industries, it is vital for organizations to develop strategies to keep up with this transformation under time pressure. According to Boston Consultancy Group (2015), the digitalization strategies of organizations will determine who will gain and lose in the process ahead. A few suggestions for the steps to be taken are presented below.

- *Understanding the root of the problem may be the first thing to define the customer's true wish.* The answer must be found for how to use digitalization to meet the real demands of customers and solve their problems.
- *Must be mentally prepared.* Being aware of the danger of disruption, it is necessary to develop a digital strategy. Organizations should look for the answer to the question "How can digitalization disrupt my industry and business." Identifying risks makes threats easy to see, and organizations develop awareness of the need to leave their comfort zone.
- *It is necessary to focus on business models.* It is true that digitization increases efficiency. This causes organizations to pay attention to the digitalization of only individual units, which leaves organizations only to efficiency-related issues, which is completely wrong. Digitalization requires developing new business models. For this, it is useful to consider the following questions mentally. How are new benefits provided to customers with digitalization, what kind of benefits are offered to new target groups? Where and with which

products to start digitalization? How does digitization change our processes, new marketing strategies and our understanding of creating value?

- *Your strategy processes should be open to communication with the environment.* It is still unknown where the ideas that shape the future will come from. Ninety percent of business innovations are derived from models transferred from the external environment or shape change. The main rule is that all kinds of inner and outer wisdom should be used without forgetting self-competence (Kohler, 2016, p. 351).

4.4 Conclusion

The aim of this study is to explore the phenomenon of digital strategy. As seen in the literature, it is clear that digitalization has not only bright but also dark sides. In order for organizations to see the dark side of digitalization at minimum level, it is perhaps the most basic requirement that they align their digital strategies with organizational strategy and business models without ignoring the holistic strategy of the organization. As a summary we can call it compatible digital strategy with organizational strategy.

This study provides important information for both academic field and practitioners. It offers a comprehensive understanding of future research for the academic world and strategy development for practitioners. It offers a wide perspective to organizations seeking digitalization by showing the other side of the coin. It may be concluded some remarks from the literature review to understand the features of a compatible digital strategy. It is clear that it can vary from organization to organization, but the following can be said as a common theme.

Considering that everything digital moves fast, organizations need to be at the same speed. What is meant by the speed in organizations is to have a strategy that ensures the adaptation of technology and flexibility of the workforce. Digital transformation requires organizations to abandon their existing hierarchical structures and instead create self-organized, loosely connected structures that can respond to destructive formations. In addition to small agile structures, it is important to have organizational agility when necessary.

Given that digital transformation is a risky process, it is obvious that the organization has a culture that encourages risk-taking and autonomy. In terms of social structure, digital is perceived as a fundamental transition of the "digital" society in which the technologies used by the generations deeply rooted in society. From this point of view, digital transformation does not include hard issues but also soft issues.

There may be the possibility of encountering the dark side, while defining the scope of digitalization. Focusing on new products and new customers rather than cost efficiency should be a priority. Having bold marginal strategies including digitization of products and services, digitalization of distribution channels, and dealing with multiple strategies simultaneously from these strategies.

Paradoxically, the focus of digital strategy and digital transformation is people and the network of organization. The organization needs people outside the organization who can establish new types of partnerships and employees with a vision that can adapt to the rapidly developing environment. While in traditional strategies the timing and speed of product launch can be determined by a single organization, it now needs to be coordinated with the partners in the product network.

References

Amit, R., & Schoemaker, P. (1993). Strategic Assets and Organizational Rent. *Strategic Management Journal*, 14(1), 33–46.

Arons, M.D.S., Van Den Driest, F., & Weed, K. (2014). The Ultimate Marketing Machine. *Harvard Business Review*, 92, 54–63.

Banker, R. D., Hu, N., Pavlou, P. A., & Luftman, J. (2011). CIO Reporting Structure, Strategic Positioning, and Firm Performance. *MIS Quarterly*, 35, 487–504.

BCG (2015). *Industry 4.0. The Future of Productivity and Growth in Manufacturing Industries*. Boston, MA: BCG.

Berger, P., & Ofek, E. (1995). Diversification's Effect on Firm Value. *Journal of Financial Economics*, 37(1), 39–65.

Bharadwaj, A., El Sawy, O. A., Pavlou, P. A., & Venkatraman, N. (2013). Digital Business Strategy: Toward a Next Generation of Insights. *MIS Quarterly*, 37, 471–482.

Buvat, J., Kvj, S., & Sumit, C. (2017). Domino's Pizza: Writing the Recipe for Digital Mastery. Paris: Cap Gemini Consulting Digital Master Series.

Castells, M. (2010). *End of Millennium* (Vol. 3). Wiley.

Coase, R. (1937). The Nature of the Firm. *Economica*, 4(16), 386–405.

Easley, D., & Kleinberg, J. (2010). *Networks, Crowds, and Markets: Reasoning about a Highly Connected World*. Cambridge, UK: Cambridge University Press.

Evans, D. S., Hagiu, A., & Schmalensee, R. (2008). *Invisible Engines: How Software Platforms Drive Innovation and Transform Industries*. Cambridge, MA: MIT Press.

Fitzgerald, M., Kruschwitz, N., Bonnet, D., & Welch, M. (2014). Embracing Digital Technology: A New Strategic Imperative. *MIT Sloan Management Review*, 55(2), 1.

Gable, G. (2010). Strategic Information Systems Research: An Archival Analysis. *Journal of Strategic Information Systems*, 19(1), 3–16.

Grover, V., & Kohli, R. (2013). Revealing Your Hand: Caveats in Implementing Digital Business Strategy. *MIS Quarterly*, 37, 655–662.

Hax, A. C. (1990). Redefining the Concept of Strategy and the Strategy Formation Process. *Planning Review*, 18(3), 34–39.

Hax, A. C., & Majluf, N. S. (1988). The Concept of Strategy and the Strategy Formation Process. *Interfaces*, 18(3), 99–109.

Hess, T., Matt, C., Wiesböck, F., & Benlian, A. (2016). Options for Formulating a Digital Transformation Strategy. *MIS Quarterly Executive*, 15(2), 123–139.

Jarzabkowski, P., Balogun, J., & Seidl, D. (2007). Strategizing: The Challenges of a Practice Perspective. *Human Relations*, 60(1), 5–27.

Kane, G. C., Palmer, D., Phillips, A. N., Kiron, D., & Buckley, N. (2015). Strategy, Not Technology, Drives Digital Transformation. *MIT Sloan Management Review and Deloitte University Press*, 14(1–25).

Keen, P., & Williams, R. (2013). Value Architectures for Digital Business: Beyond the Business Model. *MIS Quarterly*, 37(2), 643–647.

Klein, R., & Rai, A. (2009). Interfirm Strategic Information Flows in Logistics Supply Chain Relationships. *MIS Quarterly*, 33(4), 735–762.

Kohler, T. (2016). Corporate Accelerators: Building Bridges between Corporations and Startups. *Business Horizons*, 59(3), 347–357.

Kurzweil, R. (2012). *How to Create a Mind. The Secret of Human Thought Revealed.* New York: Viking Adult.

McGee, D., (2013). https://www.gartner.com/en/documents/2623616.

Malone, T., Laubacher, R., & Johns, T. (2011). The Big Idea: The Age of Hyperspecialization. *Harvard Business Review*, 89(7/8), 1–11.

Majchrzak, A., & Malhotra, A. (2013). Towards an Information Systems Perspective and Research Agenda on Crowdsourcing for Innovation. *Journal of Strategic Information Systems*, 22(4), 257–268.

Matt, C., Hess, T., & Benlian, A. (2015). Digital Transformation Strategies. *Business & Information Systems Engineering*, 57(5), 339–343.

Mintzberg, H. (1978). Patterns in Strategy Formation. *Management Science*, 24(9), 934–948.

Mintzberg, H. (1987). The Strategy Concept I: Five Ps for Strategy. *California Management Review*, 30(1), 11–24.

Mithas, S., Tafti, A., & Mitchell, W. (2013). How a Firm's Competitive Environment and Digital Strategic Posture Influence Digital Business Strategy. *MIS Quarterly*, 37, 511–536.

Mocker, M., & Teubner, A. (2005). Towards a Comprehensive Model of Information Strategy. *ECIS 2005 Proceedings*, p. 62.

Negroponte, N. (1995). The Digital Revolution: Reasons for Optimism. *The Futurist*, 29(6), 68.

OECD. (2012). *Machine-to-Machine Communications: Connecting Billions of Devices*. OECD Digital Economy Papers, No. 192, OECD Publishing. Retrieved September 22, 2020, http://www.oecd-ilibrary.org/science-and-technology/machine-to-machine-communications_5k9gsh2gp043-en.

Osterwalder, A., & Pigneur, Y. (2010). *Business Model Generation. A Handbook for Visionaries, Game Changers, and Challengers*. Hoboken, NJ: Wiley.

Oxford English Dictionary (OED). (2014). https://www.oed.com/.

Pagani, M. (2013). Digital Business Strategy and Value Creation: Framing the Dynamic Cycle of Control Points. *MIS Quarterly*, 37, 617–632.

Pardo, A. & Etay, C.(2014). Movies and Screens: The Spanish Audience's Choice. *Communication & Society*, 27(4), 131–145.

Peppard, J., & Breu, K. (2003). Beyond Alignment: A Coevolutionary View of the Information Systems Strategy Process. *ICIS 2003 Proceedings*, p. 61.

Peppard, J., & Ward, J. (2004). Beyond Strategic Information Systems: Towards an IS Capability. *The Journal of Strategic Information Systems*, 13(2), 167–194.

Powell, T. C., & Dent-Micallef, A. (1997). Information Technology as Competitive Advantage: The Role of Human, Business, and Technology Resources. *Strategic Management Journal*, 18(5), 375–405.

Reich, B. H., & Benbasat, I. (2000). Factors that Influence the Social Dimension of Alignment between Business and Information Technology Objectives. *MIS Quarterly*, 24, 81–113.

Rothmann, W., & Koch, J.(2014). Creativity in Strategic Lock-ins: The Newspaper Industry and the Digital Revolution. *Technological Forecasting & Social Change*, 83, 66–83.

Schuchmann, D., & Seufert, S. (2015). Corporate Learning in Times of Digital Transformation: A Conceptual Framework and Service Portfolio for the Learning Function in Banking Organisations. *International Journal of Advanced Corporate Learning (iJAC)*, 8(1), 31–39.

Shirky, C., (2008). *Here Comes Everybody: How Change Happens when People Come Together.* London: Penguin Books.

Stolterman, E., & Fors, A. C.(2004). Information Technology and the Good Life. In B. Kaplan et al. (Eds.), *Information Systems Research: Relevant Theory and Informed Practice*. London: Kluwer Academic Publishers.

Tams, S., Grover, V., & Thatcher, J. (2014). Modern Information Technology in an Old Workforce: Toward a Strategic Research Agenda. *Journal of Strategic Information Systems*, 23(4), 284–304.

Tsoukas, H., & Vladimirou, E. (2001). What Is Organizational Knowledge? *Journal of Management Studies*, 38(7), 973–993.

Van Dijk, J. A. (2005). *The Deepening Divide: Inequality in the Information Society*. Sage.

Von Leipzig, T., Gamp, M., Manz, D., Schöttle, K., Ohlhausen, P., Oosthuizen, G., & von Leipzig, K. (2017). Initialising Customer-Orientated Digital Transformation in Enterprises. *Procedia Manufacturing*, 8, 517–524.

Wade, M., & Hulland, J. (2004). Review: The Resource-Based View and Information Systems Research: Review, Extension, and Suggestions for Future Research. *MIS Quarterly*, 28(1), 107–142.

Wagner, E. L., & Newell, S. (2007). Exploring the Importance of Participation in the Post-implementation Period of an ES Project: A Neglected Area. *Journal of the Association for Information Systems*, 8(10), 32.

Weill, P., & Woerner, S. (2015). Thriving in an Increasingly Digital Ecosystem. *MIT Sloan Management Review*, 56(4), 27–34.

Westerman, G., Bonnet, D., & McAfee, A. (2014). *Leading Digital – Turning Technology into Business Transformation*. Boston, MA: HBR Press.

Zammuto, R., Griffith, T., Majchrzak, A., Dougherty, D., & Faraj, S., (2007). Information Technology and the Changing Fabric of Organization. *Organization Science*, 18(5), 749–762.

Serkan Yeşilyurt and Menevşe Özdemir Dilidüzgün

5. THE DARK SIDE OF DIGITAL FINANCE

Abstract Over the last five decades, finance has undergone a period of digital transformation, including digitization and data transformation. Today, finance is not only the world's most globalized segment, but also among the most digitized. This process is evident across four major areas: the emergence of global wholesale markets, a spike in financial technology startups since 2008, an unprecedented digital transformation in the financial sector of developing countries (especially in China), and the growing role played in financial services by large technology firms (TechFin) as well as increasing real-time interconnections. The Digital Financial Process Transformation carries with it systemic changes. This improvement has optimistic, but also detrimental, consequences in the form of new threats. Although finance and technology have always collaborated and assisted each other, there have been extraordinary changes over the time after the 2008 Global Financial Crisis, especially in terms of the pace of change and the scale of new entrants. Pace of transition can be seen in particular in the position of emerging technology, also summarized as the ABCD framework: artificial intelligence ("AI"), blockchain, cloud and technology, which are rapidly co-evolving with finance. Many would add mobile Internet and Internet of Things ("IoT") to this framework as well (Buckley, 2019). We conclude that financial stability (illegal activities, fraud, laundering of illicit money, terrorism financing)

Keywords: *FinTech, digital finance, digital technologies, blockchain, RegTech*

In the digital age we are in, technology has taken its place among the indispensable elements of today's world. A world without smartphones, data providing systems that enable us to communicate quickly and easily with long distances, robot processors, AI and cognitive machine learning has become a fearful and distant dream for all of us. Business life has become one of the parties that has taken the biggest share from the information technology cake that affects every field. According to Masino (1999), in today's world sectors survive as long as they keep up with technological developments and technological developments can cause some sectors to disappear. The financial sector is one of the sectors that have to keep up with technological developments. Digital finance, which means the widespread use of technology in the financial sector and services, forces the existing traditional financial system with less costly and easy-to-access services of companies equipped in the field of financial technology (FinTech), making it inevitable to make innovation a part of their daily operations (Schwab, 2016). In recent years, new business models have emerged with the development of financial technologies. However, there is not a lot of research about the development of these technologies and adaption of the businesses, especially small and medium-sized enterprises (SMEs) (Herdinata et al., 2019). Finance and technology have been going hand in hand and assist each other especially after 2008 crisis, and new entrants and changes are popping out rapidly every day. Of course the digital transformation causes some systematic changes while bringing some risks.

Over the last five decades, finance has undergone a period of digital transformation, including digitization and data transformation. Today, finance is not only the world's most globalized segment, but also among the most digitized. This process is evident across four major areas: the emergence of global wholesale markets, a spike in financial technology startups since 2008, an unprecedented digital transformation in the financial sector of developing countries (especially in China), and the growing role played in financial services by large technology firms (TechFin) as well as increasing real-time interconnections. The Digital Financial Process Transformation carries with it systemic changes. This improvement have optimistic, but also detrimental, consequences in the form of new threats. Although finance and technology have always collaborated and assisted each other, there have been extraordinary changes over the time after the 2008 Global Financial Crisis, especially in terms of the pace of change and the scale of new entrants. Pace of transition can be seen in particular in the position of emerging technology, also summarized as the ABCD framework: AI, blockchain, cloud and technology, which are rapidly co-evolving with finance. Many would add mobile Internet and Internet of Things (IoT) to this framework as well (Buckley, 2019). In the modern period of FinTech, this long-term financial digitization and code-fixing phase has gradually merged with similar developments, including big code and AI, distributed ledgers and blockchain, initial coin offerings ("ICOs"), smart contracts, regulatory technology ("RegTech") and digital identification.

In the current FinTech era, two key patterns stand out. The first is the level of transformation powered by the commoditization of technologies, big data processing, computer learning and AI. The second is the growing number and range of potential entrants to the finance market, including established technologies and e-commerce firms. Much of the discussion to date has centered on the general direction that technologized financial services will follow and how they will be governed. Significant attention has also been extended to the implications of FinTech on banks and the financial processing market, particularly the disruptive impacts of crowdfunding and crowd-lending on traditional intermediaries. But the darker side of digital financial transition can be unsettling: digital financial transition faces many threats and obstacles. This is the subject of this chapter.

This chapter proceeds, in section 2, with a framework of analysis of possible risks. The regulations will be discussed in section 3 and section 4 concludes, arguing for the need for coordinated approaches related with financial technologies and its use cases at international levels.

5.1 Finance, Technology and Finance

The concept of FinTech was formed by the combination of the words finance and technology. According to Demirdöğen (2019), financial technologies are divided into two as service-based and technology-only. While crowdfunding, new generation banking, insurtech and mobile payment systems are creating service-based FinTech; big data, blockchain, cloud computing, AI create technology-based FinTech. In order to develop financial technology, FinTech startups should be evaluated holistically within an ecosystem. In the subsystems of this ecosystem: Government policies, regulators, supervisors and legal regulations, financial structure, investors, financial institutions, consumers (users), demand, entrepreneurs (technology companies), new technologies, talented workforce, universities, incubation centers, accelerators, organizations and infrastructure quality.

Lee and Shin (2018) defined five elements in the financial technology ecosystem:

According to Bayram and Gözkonan (2019), the dominant factors of this ecosystem are FinTech startups. According to their field of activity, they can classified as follows: asset management, crediting, crowdfunding, payment systems (mobile payment), insurance and cryptocurrency. The second element of the system is technology developers like blockchain, machine learning, AI, IoT and virtual and augmented reality. Blockchain technology has begun to touch many different areas in our lives. The idea of keeping a database where peer-to-peer, secure and cannot changeable old records, it creates new use cases for blockchain. Blockchain is already being used in many different sectors and it came into our lives with Bitcoin, can now be used in a wide range of financial and non-financial areas. We will see the new areas of use of blockchain in 2020 thanks to the developments in FinTech and 5Gs coming into our lives. With the integration of blockchain into the FinTech applications, we are currently

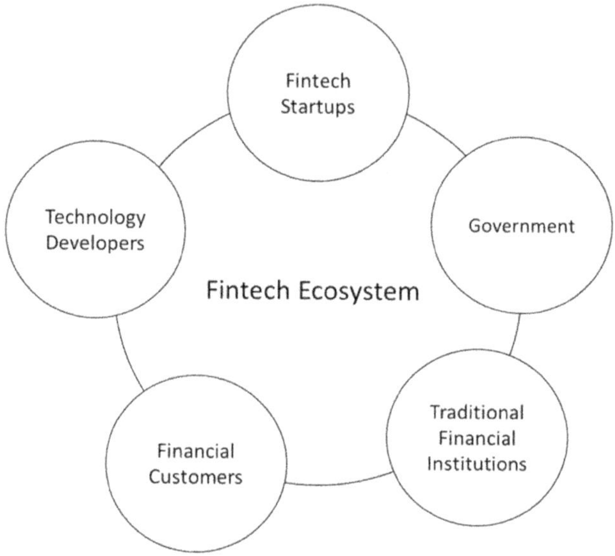

Fig. 5.1: FinTech ecosystem

using, there will be a big leap in this field. With more devices connected to the Internet in 2020, data security will become even more critical. Since all the work will be done over the Internet, some steps should be taken for mutual trust. Sharing economy will begin to enter our lives in many different areas. We cannot solve all problems with blockchain, if there is a trust problem between people who have to do business with each other on the Internet, it is thought that this problem can be solved if we can use blockchain.

FinTech presents fruitful opportunities for the future of course but at the same time it proposes risks and threats. For example, distributed ledger technology (blockchain) which supports crypto assets can allow more rapid and inexpensive transactions, however, this technology can be used for illegal activities (Lagarde, 2018) that's why the third element in the ecosystem must be regulation and supervision. Regulators must conserve investors against fraud, laundering of illicit money, terrorism financing while ensuring the financial stability. Governments have provided a positive regulatory environment for FinTech since the 2008 financial crisis. Depending on the national economic development plans, different governments implement different levels of control and regulation (licensing financial services, lowering capital adequacy levels, tax incentives) so that FinTech initiatives can create FinTech innovations and achieve global financial competition.

According to Buckley et al. (2019), two big trends emerge in the ongoing FinTech development. The first is the pace of change caused by the commoditization of technology like AI, machine learning, big data analytics and AI. The latter one is the plurality of new comers together with former e-commerce and technology companies. They advocate that the attention should be focused on the regulation of technologized financial services and companies. For example, in 2019, Facebook disclosed that it will establish a consortium to form Libra which is a new cryptocurrency to be generated and managed by a new global electronic payment network, combined with a digital identity infrastructure run by Facebook.

The public declaration by Facebook of Libra had the blast effect on the cryptocurrency business. Similarly, the industry would be experiencing a major bottleneck if Libra fizzles out as a consequence of failure to secure all necessary approvals from financial institutions, policymakers and legislators who are keen to revolt Libra headfirst to prosecute Facebook with a dark history of privacy infringement and user data misuse. According to Taskinsoy (2019), while Facebook cites Libra as a permitted disperse blockchain, however this is far from being valid since Libra is a non-minimizable cryptocurrency regardless of having computational solutions to the trouble of dual allocation. Libra cryptocurrency is a revolutionary innovation; Libra blockchain, like in any unruly technology, poses some dangers. Efficaciously, Facebook targets to establish an electronic payment system form on a payment tool allied to lawful money pools ("stablecoin") enabling it to monetize the intercommunications of its users (Zetzsche et al., 2019). This outline lays emphasis on the risks brought by digital financial transformation like hack of new currency, privacy risk, data security risk, risk of Facebook's takeover of financial system by virtue of Lira, etc. Suck perils should be main deliberations for financial regulation. Initially, Libra blockchain will be regulated by the Libra Association as an illegitimate centralized power, initially consisting of twenty-eight private authorizing affiliates, each of whom will serve as a validator to ensure the integrity of Libra (Taskinsoy, 2019).

Buckley et al. (2019) categorizes financial regulation into four major classes: financial stability, financial forthrightness, customer protection and financial market functions. Financial stability may be perceived as prevention of crises while applicable operator of the financial structure at the same time. Financial forthrightness (transparency) is geared to avoiding illegal behavior and gaining advantage from financial markets like money laundering, terrorist funding, coordinated attacks by international criminal groups and even by the state. Customer protection concentrates on structures designed to avoid customer exploitation. Financial performance, growth and inclusion concentrate on how the successful functioning and position of the financial system can be promoted and improved.

5.2 FinTech and Dark Side of It: Possible Risks in Financial Areas

We will highlight many of the key risk areas for the dark side of the finance which named as cybersecurity risk, data protection and privacy risk, data security risk, financial institution risk, technological infrastructure risk, threats to competition (Buckley et al., 2019). Technology concerns have historically been included in the sense of operational risk, which has been identified as one primary type of financial risk, along with credit risk, market risk and legal risk. Technology risks may occur in the institutional context and in the interrelationships of institutions (Bank for International Settlements, 2017). More importantly, technical developments have the potential to directly affect the trust and stability of the financial sector. Financial steadiness regulation had developed as a fundamental governing action, concentrating on description, forestalling and administration of systemic risk before 2008 financial crisis. In general, the emphasis was on the banking scope and especially in the framework of scale of specific organizations and payment scheme (Douglas, 2007). In the aftermath of global financial crises of 2008, there is an overall agreement that systematic risk consistently the consequence of the scale of financial mediator and there is a general awareness that the scale of mediators and the network of multilateral relations are main causes of systematic risk (Bernanke, 2010).

Cybersecurity has become one of the main sources of structural risk in the financial sector, by virtue of digital financial transformation and one of the main interested fields of financial authorities. The basic level of cyber threat emerges from the high pace and pattern of technological growth and the implementation in communication circuits. Cybersecurity is the primary cause of systematic risk together with most critical national security concerns. According to company reports, in 2018, cyberattacks have raised 15 % compared to 2017 and day by day they are growing gradually in intensity and duration (European Court of Auditors, 2019). Cybersecurity risk can therefore be regarded as a modern origin of conventional risk with likely disastrous results. For example the hack case which took place in a Russian bank resulting in implementation of $400 million in trades has shifted the currency rate of USD/Ruble by 15 %. Although financial institutions have concentrated on all types of fraud and theft hazard for a long time, computerization and globalization create the possibility for just pure fraud and corruption to take on a much larger level. For example: An attacker may theoretically steal or target all wallets and workplaces of several companies in different territories simultaneously, instead of stealing one account, office or company (Buckley et al., 2019). The problem here is bigger because hackers have a diverse set of motives.

The increasing reliance on nuanced, unreplaced digitalized centers of information technology is opposed by FinTech's growing amount of external facing, boosting cyber visibility. Hacking attacks can manipulate these security bugs to interrupt payroll processing, illegitimate custodian banks data, or paralyze financial system-based networks. Although these are low-risk occurrences, if not regulated, their occurrence would have potentially high implications able to escalate into financial instability. Cyber risk emerges from the great pace and type of technology advancement and the implementation in finance of electronic systems. The increasing shift to cloud computing produces more clustered data centers with less variety of applications, giving greater security requirements. Intracellular risks to such centers arise from internal company or customer data breaches, and illegitimate access to networks by or through users or staff. External risks include violations of connecting with other third party networks, including using special login details that have been illegally obtained to reach data and conduct business dealings (Boer and Vazquez, 2017). Another problem arises from cyber-governance delays and discrepancies in different countries. Although digital world is a high-speed, unshakeable global network, its regulations are blurred, with substantial differences at best, and at worst moral conflicts among different actors. Strong legislative conditions at national level, especially in the less developed inconsistencies expose the weakness of smaller private and public agencies, exposing the larger structure to the descend consequences of the breaches. Efforts to minimize such sector specific disparities are embryonic and have not yet been proved for their effect (European Court of Auditors, March 2019). Other threats are related to the integration of public safety and cyber-domain financial sustainability. While data protection has been traditionally interpreted as a duty of the government, aimed at securing internal essential framework and virtual worlds from events of public safety, increasingly integrated data and transaction streams need an expansion of the mandate. Data protection is usually thought developed where conventional essential services is included, but the explosion of data and cash flow facilitated by FinTech can generate a hazardous interconnectedness that attempts to divert participant focus away from virtual flexibility. In order to mitigate the mentioned threats, Buckley et al. (2019) recommend widening the reach of virtual-incident possibilities globally, including a range of FinTechs not only to determine device vulnerabilities and expenses, but also to explain the classification of obligation, which may be helpful in mitigating confusion in the event of a web-caused problem and helping to facilitate a shared legislative structure.

Besides cybersecurity, the progressively key position of data in the financial sector underscores the second significant issue: data security. In various countries different standards are being created, in part reflecting radically various attitudes to society. The United States, China and the EU are the popular models of differing permissible ways to data use, control and security (World Development Report, 2020). According to Carstens (2018) credit and solvency are triggered by the scale of other FinTechs, and implementing investor driven risks. Commercial banks can turn small deposits into big loans, whereas FinTech will focus on a combination of in-house sources, syndicated loans and originating trustification. Usage of auxiliary non-conventional banking data to assess credit risk can inject distinct layers of risk controlled by the magnitude of the data examples accessible thus avoiding standardized regulatory answers.

Information security and protection hazard contrast from cybersecurity in that they apply to the use and reality of data gathered rather than its defense. Regulators should also regularly review the state service for vulnerabilities in honesty, re-identification threats, etc. That needs adequate resources and empowers to examine the diverse volumes of data. As soon as it is examined, judicial risk assessment systems can be developed and revised. According to Vemou and Maria (2019), close to cyberactivity, it is through networks of data experts sharing methodologies that the most efficient way to promote more successful data analyses. They advocate propping available attempts and strengthening public-private corporations to truly comprehend risk factors and occurrences able to draw condemnation from stakeholders, in particular FinTechs with possible effects on organizational multi-border confidence.

Additionally recent risks from virtual era and from fresh financial organizations, the creation of new models of digital financial frameworks also creates new risks. The presence of emerging financial players such as FinTechs and BigTech, which refers to big international technology companies that have a competitive edge in digital technology, pose possible issues including cybersecurity and information security (Frost et al., 2019). Great amount of FinTechs do not aim to challenge available mediators; instead they would like to work together as customers and pursue mediators and this is where the real innovation in FinTech occurs – and at a brisk speed.

5.3 Regulations in FinTech

FinTech are being increasingly the center of today world. Their flurry of activities raises concerns about what kind of financial world will arise as a result of the digital transition. The key questions are about the position that traditional financial institutions can play, but above all about the potential challenges that the new policies present for financial services customers. Until now, conventional financial institutions have primarily reacted by partnering with startups in FinTech instead of by attempting to buy them. The digital revolution presents the finance industry with a tremendous growth opportunity. It is important that the required regulatory reforms should not make it impossible to innovate while at the same time maintaining the consistency that the infrastructure requires in order to satisfy consumer demands and uncertainties and difficulties. Traditional financial institutions and FinTech startups face regulatory hurdles in terms of capital requirements, anti-money laundering, and privacy and protection. Traditional financial institutions and FinTech startups face different regulatory requirements depending on the type of financial services they offer. However, the cost of meeting regulatory requirements and competing against FinTech startups may be important. For example, most banks operate under some type of fractional-reserve banking system. There are strict and nuanced rules for what form of lending should be performed on the basis of the capital owned by a conventional financial institution that does not apply to a lending FinTech (Lee and Shin, 2018).

Trade and community have evolved dramatically from technological innovations. The age of the digital economy was launched by a new finance system in the form of financial technology (FinTech). At the same time, regulatory responses are expected to inherent threats to technological advances, such as technical hazards, information asymmetry, and even structural threats. However, obsolete compliance methods, archaic financial rules, and restrictive regulatory principles make it impossible for conventional financial intermediary-based on legislation to adjust to the new world of decentralized financial transactions. Data management technology led legislation may help to overcome the inefficiency and inefficiency of conventional financial laws and improve effective enforcement of the rights and interests of financial customers. This new regulatory model attempts to create a structure implemented for all parties (i.e., regulators and financial institutions governed by the new regulatory model) with fair access to blockchain transactions information for regulation, smart real-time monitoring as well as a platform for the advancement of regulatory technologies. This complex and scalable financial regulation structure will manage the challenges of FinTech effectively (Dong and Li, 2019).

It is clear that Regulation Technology (RegTech) is not a part of FinTech, rather they are related but in different. It is argued that RegTech is the adaptation and use of technology to help financial services to well understand and apply with regulatory requirements more effectively. The financial regulations are claimed to be technology-driven and data-driven regulations which seems more effective than others. The development of a technology-driven regulation has two root causes. First, FinTech innovation risks – such as technical risk, extreme knowledge asymmetry, regulatory risk, systematic risk and structural risk – these risks require regulators to take proactive steps to protect the entire financial sector. Second, existing regulatory structures, which rely on financial institution thresholds (access regulations), are inadequate and counterproductive for FinTech regulations. These model well represents Fig. 2 below:

In a technology-driven regulatory model, however, regulators may use technology to collect timely and efficient data, which converts enforcement from passive monitoring to successful simultaneous information collection. Both regulators and controlled must have fair access to information, allowing knowledge exchange and creating an open, collaborative community of regulators and controlled agencies. Many organizations are expected to report records, including not only financial institutions and credit channels, but also business and government agencies. Thus, the regulatory model will be changed from one of the relevant stakeholders' single supervision to one of co-governance, and a flat regulatory system will replace hierarchical regulation. Consequently, technology-driven regulation encourages a different form of partnership to be established between regulators and controlled institutions where managers at companies, financial intermediaries, and customers are equal participants. Through using accurate and reliable messaging, regulators could consider the priorities of FinTech companies, and businesses could appreciate legislation from their own viewpoint (Yang and Li, 2019).

5.4 Conclusion

At the end of 2008 financial crisis, the financial services sector has started a period of accelerated to the new transformation called as digital and technological transformation. New market models focused on converging technology advances question the status quo of a long-established and conservative

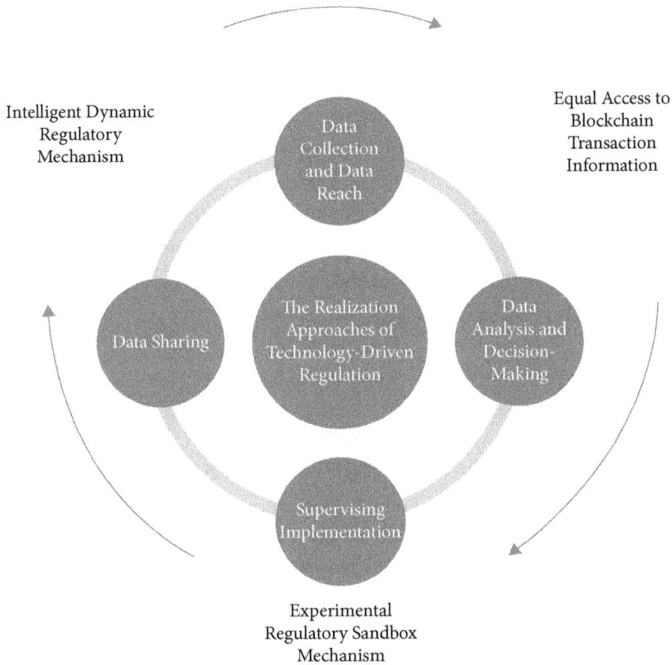

Fig. 5.2: Mechanisms of technology-driven regulation. Source: Dong and Li 2019

industry. It concludes that the transformational trends in the financial services sector would most likely boost and extend access to finance for businesses and individuals, as well as increase formalization and financial inclusion. This digitalization peaked during COVID-19 term, the spread of COVID-19 and related government lockdowns have led to between a 24 % and 32 % increase in the relative rate of daily downloads of finance mobile applications (Fu and Mishra, 2020). However, some obstacles and threats that may impede the development of the FinTech industry, it is called as the dark side of it. The vulnerabilities regarding technology threats in the regulatory framework are close to those we encountered prior to the 2008 Global Financial Crisis with regard to macroeconomic threats. These shortcomings include lack of awareness, mandate gaps, regulatory gaps, lack of regulator cooperation, asymmetric information, lack of financial mediators and regulators expertise. The lack of adequate and timely legislation, the lack of access to high quality and accessible Internet infrastructure (broadband access) and the unforeseen and highly disruptive developments that may occur from the payment region. Cybersecurity, fraud, laundering of illicit money, terrorism financing are the abuse usage of digital transformed environment (Ketterer, 2017).

The world has become more dangerous with FinTech turning tech risk into a main factor of risk levels. Sooner or later, the latest technological risk would transform into financial risk. In its primary role, a regulatory framework that remains until financial threats have eventuated as long-term consequences of technology risk have fallen. Regulatory authorities have to consider the unpredictable rather than fear it, and establish a level of tech sophistication that only the big data-driven corporations suit.

References

Basel Committee on Banking Supervision (December 2017). Basel III: A global regulatory framework for more resilient banking systems. https://www.bis.org/publ/bcbs189.pdf.

Bayram, E., & Gözkonan, U. H. (2019). Türkiye'de İslami Fintek İş Modelinin Swot Analizi. Business and Organization Research Izmir (International Conference).

Boer, M. & Vazquez, J. (2017). *Cyber Security & Financial Stability: How Cyber-Attacks Could Materially Impact the Global Financial System.* Institute of International Finance.

Buckley, R. P., Douglas, W. A., Zetzsche, D. A., & Selga, E. (2019). The Dark Side of Digital Financial Transformation: The New Risks of FinTech and the Rise of TechRisk, EBI Working Paper.

Chen, Mark A, Wu, Qinki, Yang, Baozhong (2019) How Valuable Is Fintech Innovation? *The Review of Financial Studies*, 32(5), 2062–2106.

Challenges to Effective EU Cybersecurity Policy (European Court of Auditors March 2019). https://www.eca.europa.eu/Lists/ECADocuments/BRP_CYBERSECURITY/BRP_CYBERSECURITY_EN.pdf, accessed 4 September 2020.

Demirdöğen, Y. (2019). FinTek Ekosistemi için Gerekli Düzenlemeler (REGTEK). *Süleyman Demirel Üniversitesi Vizyoner Dergisi*, 10(24), 311–321.

Dong, Y., & Li M. (2019). Evolutionary Approaches and the Construction of Technology-Driven Regulations. *Emerging Markets Finance and Trade.*

Douglas, W. A. (2007) Financial Stability, Economic Growth, and the Role of Law.

Frost, J., Gambacorta, L., Huang, Y., Shin, H. S., & Zbinden, P. (2019). BigTech and the Changing Structure of Financial Intermediation, BIS Working Papers No. 779.

Fu, F., & Mishra, M. (2020). The Global Impact of COVID-19 on FinTech Adoption. Swiss Finance Institute Research Paper No. 20–38.

Herdinata et al. (2019). Effect of Organızatıonal Competence, Organızatıonal Support, and Organızatıonal Productıvıty towards Adoptıon of Fınancıal Technology. *Journal of Applied Management* (JAM) 17(4).

Ketterer, A. H. (2017). Digital Finance, New Times, New Challenges, New Opportunities, Inter-American Development Bank Discussion Paper, No. IDB-DP-501.

Lagarde, C. (2018). A Regulatory Approach to FinTech. *Finance & Development*, 9–10. International Monetary Fund.

Lee, I., & Shin, Y. J. (2018). FinTech: Ecosystem, Business Models, Investment Decisions, and Challenges. *Business Horizons*, 61(1), 35–46.

Schwab, K. (2016). *Dördüncü Sanayi Devrimi. (Çev.) Zülfü Dicleli.* İstanbul: Optimist Yayınları.

Taskinsoy, John, Is Facebook's Libra Project Already a Miscarriage? (August 15, 2019). Available at SSRN: https://ssrn.com/abstract=3437857

Testimony before the Financial Crisis Enquiry Commission (2 September 2010). Causes of the Recent Financial and Economic Crisis. Washington, DC: United States Congress (Ben Bernanke). https://www.federalreserve.gov/newsevents/testimony/bernanke20100902a.htm.

Vemou, K., & Maria, K. (2019). Evaluating Privacy Impact Assessment Methods: Guidelines and Best Practice. Information & Computer Security. https://www.emerald.com/insight/content/doi/10.1108/ICS-04-2019-0047/full/html, accessed 2 September 2020.

World Bank (2019). *World Development Report 2020: Trading for Development in the Age of Global Value Chains*. The World Bank, p. 245. http://elibrary.worldbank.org/doi/book/10.1596/978-1-4648-1457-0, accessed 24 October 2019.

Zetzsche, D. A., Buckley, R. P.,& Douglas, W. A. (2019). Regulating Libra, EBI Working Paper. www.ssrn.com/abstract=3414401.

Mustafa Sundu

6. NEGATIVE CONSEQUENCES OF DIGITALIZATION IN WORKPLACES: CHALLENGES FOR LEADERS AND MANAGERS

Abstract As the technology improve, it affects all aspects of human life and even all planet. Today information technologies deeply shape the human culture and business environment. Digitization of products or things bring a transformation to all way of doing business. Digital transformation offers many benefits to businesses such as operational excellence, cost reduction, effective customer relationship and full integration or partnership with other firms. Along with these benefits, digital technology may pose some challenges. This section discusses all aspects of the challenges posed by digital transformation and highlight vital issues for managers and leaders who are supposed to deal with these challenges.

Keywords: *Digital transformation, digital workplace, digitalization, organizational change, managerial challenges*

Since the industrial revolution, management and leadership activities has been focused the effectiveness and efficiency of business firms. Although methods and techniques has been changed, focus of managers and leaders has been always remained same, which is to survive by ensuring efficiency and effectiveness. Actually, after industrial revolution which means heavy usage of machines to manufacture mass number of products, workplaces have been completely changed. This new mass production method in which machines are used, brought a major change not only to the life of employees but also to the life of managers in the workplaces.

When industrial revolution paced at the last quarter of nineteenth century organizational and managerial issues started to be discussed by scholars of Scientific Management School and General Management Theory. Frederick Winslow Taylor (1856–1915), Henri Fayol (1841–1925), Frank and Lillian Gilbreth (1868–1924, 1878–1972), Henry Gantt (1861–1919), Ian Hamilton (1853–1947), Mary Parker Follett (1868–1933), Chester Barnard (1886– 1961), Cyril Burt (1883–1972) and Elton Mayo (1880–1949) are some of the pioneer management researchers (Drucker, 2012, pp. 22–23; Eilon, 2012, p. 254; Griffin,

2012, pp. 34–41; Rahman, 2012, pp. 96–100; Robbins & Coulter, 2012, pp. 29–34). The scientific management school developed first theories of management and leadership. First and biggest problem was to synchronize employees with machines which were firstly used for mass production. This alignment, between human and machines, was of prominent importance and need to be ensured. Researches and experiments were focusing on job and movement analysis, job description, recruitment of proper employees and job allocation. This school mostly studied micro issues. However, management and leadership principles has been suggested as well. Managers and leaders were trying to make perfect planning and applications for efficiency and effectiveness, which means to achieve higher performance but to use minimum resource. By the way, this approach ignored the individual and social issues of workplace such as motivation, employee satisfaction and job satisfaction, group dynamics, communication etc. And then conflicts aroused between managers and employees in the workplaces. These conflicts leaded inefficiency and performance failure in the business firms. From these discussions regarding workplaces a new theory has been born; Human Relations and Systems Theory (Pryor et al., 2011, p. 965; Robbins et al., 2014, p. 36). Today alignment of business, human and society to new situation due to digital transformation of industries and life is discussed once more. For sure many factors affect the emergence of a new theory. These factors vary from social facts and human culture to new technologies which are shaping community, businesses, markets and accordingly workplaces. Today, disruptive technologies such as, artificial intelligence (AI), information technologies (ITs), Internet and digitalization are shaping every aspect of human life and culture including workplaces. And this impact is not always creating a positive result. Therefore, in this chapter possible negative consequences of the new trend which is digitalization will be discussed broadly. Especially challenges for managers in the digital transformation will be highlighted.

6.1 Who Are Managers and Leaders in the Workplaces?

A broad definition of management is the use of organizational resources to achieve the organization's profit or nonprofit goals. Organizational resources can be categorized as financial, human, physical and information. Management involves many activities which need to be carried out synchronously. These activities are grouped into four main functions which are planning, organizing, leading and controlling. Managers are supposed to conduct all these functions (Drucker, 2012, pp. 159–160; Griffin, 2012, p. 121; Robbins et al., 2014, p. 8;

Robbins & Coulter, 2012, p. 9). As seen obviously leading is one of the main responsibility of managers. Managers and leaders can be perceived as different individuals according to the discussions in the literature. Indeed, manager and leader are like the two sides of a coin and embodied in one individual.

Leadership is a common word used in daily life. Members of every sector and individuals in every community have their own specific leadership definitions. There may be leadership definitions as many as the number of organizations, and most of them make sense. It is the same for the academic environment. There are plenty of leadership definitions and theories suggested by many scholars and researchers in the academic world (Banks et al., 2019, pp. 1–2). But, leadership theories can be categorized, and definitions can be made accordingly. Parallel to the improvements of management and organization theories, it can be easily seen that how leadership theories and definitions changed and get sophisticated. A common definition of leadership is to influence others to achieve a designated goal (Banks et al., 2019, pp. 1–2; Johnson & Hackman, 2018, pp. 2–19; Nahavandi, 2014, p. 3; Pfeffermann, 2019, p. 148; Robbins & Judge, 2017, pp. 421–444; Yukl, 2008, p. 19).

Both management (Kohnke, 2017, p. 73) and leadership processes involve an intense exchange of messages and emotions. Especially conflicts or good relationships arise when managers or leaders carry out activities related to leadership and control functions. All these exchanges and interactions take place at workplaces. The need for digital transformation has become an indispensable requirement for all organizations and therefore workplaces. Management, leadership and workplaces will inevitably change as organizations are transformed digitally.

6.2 Digital Transformation

The term digital is produced from the term digit which means any of the numerals from 0 to 9. This term mostly belongs to computing literature and refers to mathematical computing by using numbers. After invention of computers this calculation activity handed over to machines by human. Actually computer era started with digital computing made by computers (Ceruzzi, 2013, pp. 1–3). By the way digitization and digital transformation are relational but in the same time different terms (Legner et al., 2017, p. 1). Digitization is the process of converting of analog information such as, book, message, music, video or picture etc. to digital form by using digital computing technologies (Ceruzzi, 2013, pp. 1–13; Gobble, 2018, pp. 56–59; Kagerman, 2015, p. 24; Legner et al., 2017, pp. 1–3). Digitization is a technical term and process. On the contrary, digital transformation concept has much more inclusive and complex meaning which is mostly organizational and managerial. A broad definition of digital transformation is to adapt to digital economy shaped by digital technology. That means a full integration of firm to the digitalized sector in which it operates (Albach et al., 2015, pp. 3–27; Bondar et al., 2017, pp. 33–34). Digitization is a computerization and operational process while the digital transformation requires creating an innovative business value which reform a business and sometimes all industry (Gobble, 2018, p. 57). Digital transformation include all processes of adopting and using digital technologies in terms of individual, organizational, and societal contexts (Legner et al., 2017, p. 4). Regardless industry or firm, digital transformation strategies have to encompass use of technologies, changes in value creation, structural changes, and financial issues (Matt et al., 2015, p. 339).

There are many factors in the business environment force industries and organizations to be digitally transformed. Digitization of products and process creating a perfect transparency in terms of price and performance of products. Therefore, competition is getting fierce. New competitors of any size can emerge anytime anywhere in the digital world. Digitally pioneer companies will be dominant in the market. Because digitalization dramatically reduces labor and operational cost and facilitate partnerships which can add new competent to company easily. Digitalization create talent mismatch which means existing human resources do not meet the need of company. Supply chains are supposed to be integrated all around the world since digitalization ease the process. This integration need to be managed globally (Gimple et al., 2018, pp. 36–48; Hirt & Willmott, 2014, pp. 3–9). All these forces increase dynamics of change and the need for a new style of management and leadership. So, new challenges appear in all areas such as business model, human resources, partnership, strategy and technology management. In case of misleading this transformation process could bring major problems to company even totally failure of business (Kohnke, 2017, pp. 73–79). On the other hand increases of investment on digital technology (Bondar et al., 2017, p. 41) is also threatening financial balance of enterprises. Therefore digital transformation strategies must cover all aspects of the firm and it is essential to closely align the four main elements: use of technologies, changes in value creation, structural changes, and financial capability (Matt et al., 2015, p. 340).

6.3 Workplaces and Digital Workplaces

As beforementioned, main concern of managers and leaders in the organization is to achieve efficient and effective performance (Drucker, 2012, p. 18).

Naturally, they reach this goal together with employees in the facilities. Traditional working places are physical facilities such as factory buildings, offices, stores and warehouses etc. However today, there are many new ways of working distantly and asynchronously or synchronously. Therefore, definition of workplace has been widened as well. The digital workplace can be described as part of the IT infrastructure that is available for the user assigned in an organizational structure. The digital workplace environment contains software, hardware, data services and standard of procedures (Schmidt et al., 2018, p. 20).

Briefly digital workplaces are those equipped with digital devices operating on communication technology infrastructure. At first glance, it is seen as just a technology update in the organization, but this change has a great impact on people and the organization. Depending the extent, capacity and level of workplace technology, impacts on organization vary. First-level effects are expected to be on the performance of work. Second-level effects occur in the organizational roles and the work style in the organizations. Third-level effects are much more effective and create bigger change and transformation such as competency, identity and strategy even definition of organization (Baptista et al., 2020, p. 9).

Dramatic changes in technology bring a new workplace and team structure which is consisting of machines (robots, intelligent agents etc.) and human (Chakraborti et al., 2017, p. 4). Machines and human working together in the workplaces since the beginning of industrial revolution. But this time it is quite different. Because now, machines and human are autonomous and equal team members in terms of taking responsibility, making decision, allocating tasks in teaming process.

6.4 Negative Consequences of Digital Transformation in Workplaces

Digitalization inevitably reshapes products and services, workplaces, communication process and social life intensely (Gimple et al., 2018, p. 3; Gobble, 2018, pp. 56–58; Kagerman, 2015, p. 24; Larson & DeChurch, 2020, p. 1; Legner et al., 2017, p. 4; Li, 2020; Matt et al., 2015, p. 341; Oswald & Kleinemeier, 2017, p. 71; Sener & Yuksel, 2017, p. 292; Vial, 2019, pp. 119–122). The negative effects of digital transformation on workplaces can be discussed under the three main headings. First one is the managerial and organizational issues in the workplace. Second one is communication, coordination and leadership regarding problems in the workplace. Third one is the individual matters and social issues.

6.5 Managerial and Organizational Issues in the Workplace

Digitization of products is shattering market and industry boundaries (Yoo et al., 2010, p. 731). Market and industry are the one of the inputs for traditional strategic management process (Eilon, 2012, pp. 304–307; Lynch, 2015, pp. 73–83). Therefore, the traditional approach to developing competitive strategy can create major problems for the organization. This is an important source of risk for the senior management process. Digital technology adoption, digital product and market integration are emerging as new areas on which the strategic management process depends. Companies must constantly review their product platforms, technologies, core competencies and partnerships (Yoo et al., 2010, pp. 731–733). Additionally, digitization of products brings new challenge regarding ownership and partnership. So, a new approach to contract management and legal issues is of prominent importance (Yoo et al., 2012, p. 1401). Failure in contracting process can pose big problems to the business.

One of the biggest problems for leaders in the digital workplaces is to ensure a flawless communication process. Face-to-face communication is much more effective for coordination than virtual chat or video conference communication. Members of virtual teams, which operate in a digital workplace, are also generally less satisfied in their team interactions than face-to-face teams. Especially trust which is very vital issue to get a perfect team performance is also difficult to form by digital means. Another conflict source is interaction between human-robot or human-AI fueled systems in the digital workplaces. Human has been working together with machines with some extent of automation since the industry revolution. But in the digital era human machine relations are becoming similar to human-to-human relations due to smarter machines such as human like robots (Chakraborti et al., 2017, pp. 1–5) or intelligent agents.

Digital transformation is forcing organizational structure to be changed. It is not only matter of machines and human are working in the same workplaces, but machines are acting as teammate since the improvement of AI techniques. Humans can easily act proactively and properly as a team member due to human cognitive skills. They can quickly figure out team context according to team task and behaviors of teammates. Consequently, humans are able to predict proper behavior and to make decision for individual goals for the success of team. These skills are of vital importance in the coordination process of team. Machine teammates are supposed to have these skills which are crucial for being an effective and successful team. Therefore challenge in the digitally transformed workplaces in where machines and humans are working together is mostly cognitive rather than physical (Chakraborti et al., 2017, pp. 5–8). For example, backchanelling capability of robots in the communication process has a significant impact on the success of the human-robot teams in a demanding and complex task environment. Backchanneling refers to mostly behavioral and nonverbal signals without speaking by an audience in a communication process which means that the listener is actively participated into communication. Backchanneling encompasses gestures, mimics and facial expressions such as some sounds, nodding, eye contact, and orientation towards the speaking one (Jung et al., 2013, pp. 1556–1563). Naturally robots with backchanneling skills will be most probably expensive but necessary for the performance increase of human-robot teams. This is also a challenge for managers as well for robot designers.

Robots or intelligent agents have the capability of human beings such as decision making, visual perception, speech recognition and prediction due to AI applications such as machine learning, deep learning. These human like capacity make machines an equal teammate in the workplaces and every organizational process such as leadership emergence are impacted by this new fact. Leaders have to establish organizational structure and business processes which are ensuring a perfect match between human and machines (Robots, agents, computer aided systems etc.). Therefore, leaders should be able to understand human related organizational issues and in the same time new technologies. This is crucial for designing technology which is proper for the organization. The teams of intelligent machines and human pose challenges about coordination process. It is difficult to decide when the human should take responsibility and when the machine should lead the process (Larson & DeChurch, 2020, p. 13). Giving more decision authority to human in task allocation is not enough for human employee satisfaction and can yield performance failure. When human is given task allocation authority, human is prone to take more tasks than robot teammate compared to human teammate. This a planning mistake and result in dissatisfaction and performance failure of team (Gombolay et al., 2015, p. 309). Leaders should assist employees to improve their interaction with these systems and to learn new technologies in terms of capability and the extent of intelligence (Larson & DeChurch, 2020, p. 12).

Digitalized businesses and markets demand real time transactions, high efficiency, and faster delivery. These demands increase pressure and stress on personnel (Sener & Yuksel, 2017, p. 297). Stress on personnel can trigger disputes and complicate the resolution of the conflicts. Information technologies and digitalized processes offer platforms for idea exchange and collective knowledge generation inside organization. These platforms easily combine dispersed units and members of organization. Beside these benefits, this kind of transformation can bring a chaotic environment for organization in terms of traditional rules and procedures. Digital communication means such as mail, instant messaging shatter traditional hierarchy in the organizational structure (Cortellazzo et al., 2019, p. 9). If leaders cannot manage this change and create a democratic environment which ensure participative decision-making process and easy access to information, digital transformation disastrously harm the business.

Digitalization changed the way of performance measurement in the digital workplaces which is totally transparent. What task is given, when the task is fulfilled, and the success or unsuccess in the accomplishment of task is visible by everyone in the virtual collaboration tools or digital work environment (Schwarzmüller et al., 2018, p. 127). Further, due to speed and fierce competition which digitalization forces, business demand and need for faster and continuous innovation increasing as well. This is also source of stress on employees and increased job demand. Lifelong learning approach should be adopted individually and organizationally to cope with continuously increase in job demand and higher performance (Schwarzmüller et al., 2018, p. 124).

There is a trend in most organizations to digitize learning and knowledge base resources to eliminate paper waste and centralize knowledge management. As many organizations try to digitize their learning and knowledge base materials, some employees find it difficult to adapt to new technologies and learn with digital materials. The first and temporary response is mostly to get back to use paper document resources. But organizations have to begin developing digital literacy training to address these problems. Also, there are suggestions that employees have a lower desire to learn and read with digital platforms such as desktop computers. Efforts to digitize learning and knowledge base resources in the workplace need to be supported by a strategy that demonstrates the value of new technology and its benefit to employees. In addition, it would be beneficial to continue digital literacy training and equip employees with IT resources that encourage them to use (Klassen, 2019, p. 5). Otherwise, the training and learning and even knowledge management processes of the organization will be interrupted.

Dependence on IT and vulnerability of IT against cyberattacks is another challenge for managers. Privacy and security are the main concern of digital world (Vial, 2019, p. 131). Due to technical features of digital technologies it is easy to violate any privacy and any security measures. Digital transformation facilitates and force firms to combine their suppliers and product delivery channels in one body which is also integrated with the business partners as well. Fierce competition, customer demands for fast and quality necessitate industry to act as one entity. But this unity and integration highly depend on digital infrastructure which is very sensitive and difficult to secure. So, today every companies and organization need a profound cybersecurity capability and assets.

The cybersecurity of an enterprise or organization is to protect information, which is usually a valuable property of the company, to ensure the safe existence of databases as a whole, to provide timely access to information by authorized users and to prevent unauthorized access to information. Cybersecurity measures include the protection of the IT infrastructure against physical attacks and damages. Cybersecurity practices aim to make an organization more competitive and successful in a safe and secure environment. Cybersecurity includes not only technical issues, but also strategies that increase trust with shareholders, customers and stakeholders by preventing business brand damage, actual losses and business disruptions (Morris et al., 2020, p. 3). Cybersecurity breaches are costing billions of dollars to the World economy and has an increasing trend (Malatji et al., 2020, p. 1). IBM has published the Cost of Data Breach Report 2020, covering 17 countries, 17 sectors, 524 organizations and prepared by interviewing more than 3,200 people who are experts in cybersecurity. The report states that there is an average annual cost of $3.86 million per organization due to cybersecurity breaches (IBM Security, 2020, pp. 2–5). When compared to the other challenges due to digital transformation, cybersecurity is of prominent importance and should be first item in agenda of managers.

6.6 Communication, Coordination and Leadership in the Workplace

One of the biggest challenges in any digitalized sector is cooperation and coordination. Digital transformation forces firms to be integrated to other firms, suppliers and customers. This integration demands firm to constantly cope with problems about exchanging data with partners, data compatibility, system standards, service and product quality and security needs. Additionally, this integration includes linkages to customers and need of managing communication with customers pose big challenges such as coping with volatile environment, deadline violation and quality failures. Digitalization connects employees to each other and facilitate fast and effective communication which generates big amount of information (Albach et al., 2015, p. 34). This also one of the challenges which need to be managed properly.

Digital transformation requires new type of leadership and employee skills. Therefore, managers, leaders and employees must improve their skills and computer/digital literacy (Legner et al., 2017, pp. 4–5; Valentine & Stewart, 2015, p. 4520) to the level which the new generation naturally has. Today, digitalized education platforms facilitate individual or institutional education. If digital transformation cannot be achieved completely then firm can lose operational efficiency and effectiveness, even its own valuable assets. Thus, choosing leader of digital transformation is of vital importance. It remains a big question who will lead this process. Chief Information Officers (CIO) are supposed to be natural leader of digital transformation. However, leadership of CIOs and use only technical approach can cause some disputes between the other elements of firm. Therefore, it will be much more effective to design a collective management model that reflects all aspects and concerns of enterprise (Matt et al., 2015, p. 340). Such management group should have the ability to not only ask the right questions of management and advisors, they must also be competent to challenge their response and resistance (Valentine & Stewart, 2015, p. 4513). Digital transformation strategies need to be aligned with business and corporate strategies of firm. Additionally top management should provide full support for an absolute achievement (Issa et al., 2018; Matt et al., 2015, p. 340).

Leader member exchange certainly will be different in a digitally transformed environment. For example, how social media platforms will change leader member exchange is a meaningful research problem (Banks et al., 2019, pp. 1–2).

Digital technology facilitates to create multinational team with the members dispersed all around the World. However, the use of digital technology for communication or coordination between virtual team members may trigger some problems. The differences in culture, time and work style could become a nightmare for managers. Additionally, psychological safety shared by team members can solve many problems that could be arise in the workplaces. But it is difficult to create psychological safety among team members in a digital multinational environment (Larson & DeChurch, 2020, p. 5).

Digital teams and virtual organizations communicate via digital means such as instant messaging, social media means and video conferencing etc. Digital communication is the source of many challenges compared to face-to-face communication. And it becomes much more complex issue for international organizations of which elements operates in the different geographic locations and have different cultural aspects. Leading such a digital team is another challenge for managers and leaders when compared to face-to-face teams (Larson & DeChurch, 2020, pp. 4–9). Nonverbal communication types such as eye contact, mimics and gestures are important for delivering message and motivating group effectively (Luo et al., 2013, pp. 229–238; Sauppé & Mutlu, 2014, pp. 342–349; Zeki, 2009, pp. 1–7). In virtual teams, on the contrary, most communication tools are nonverbal, meaning they are written, such as instant messaging or e-mail. Although there are digital face-to-face means such as video conferencing which could be used in the digital workplaces, it cannot be assumed as a real face-to-face communication. Therefore, it is a big challenge for leaders and managers to establish an effective communication process in the digital workplaces. Leaders and managers need to figure out new ways to enhance communication effectiveness for organizational success.

Many problems that digitalization bring may be easily noticed and resolved by the managers. But there is a hidden risk which could make things worse, the impact of digital transformation to emergence process of leaders. A company which has been operating for many years has already defined processes, job descriptions, authorities and responsibilities. When this company experienced a digital transformation that means not only formal structure, but informal structure of organization will be transformed. Because being co-located and using digital communication means intensively effect the emergence of leaders. It is suggested that text-based communication ability has a significant effect on emergent leadership and quality and quantity of computer aided communication partially mediated this relation (Charlier et al., 2016, p. 14). This fact may trigger some disputes between formal leaders and followers in the organization after transformation. Because new leaders are likely to emerge in this digital environment.

6.7 Individual and Social Issues in the Workplace

Worker alienation, weak social bonding, and poor accountability are some of prominent problems which are experienced by workers in the workplace. Additionally, greater autonomy, isolation and increased job demands due to digital transformation break the work peace and job satisfaction. Therefore it is crucial that leaders provide support and help to followers such as coaching, allocating necessary resources, and assist for handling tasks (Cortellazzo et al., 2019, p. 12).

As part of the workplace health management process, digital psychological interventions for the mental well-being of workforce are becoming preferable to face-to-face interventions. The most important reason for this is that they are cost-effective, their potential to reach more individuals easily, and they secure privacy, thus preventing other employees from developing prejudices against these people. However, published evidence on the effectiveness of digital interventions contributing to the psychological health of employees is still lacking (Armaou et al., 2020, pp. 1–9). Therefore, a failure on mental well-being of employees in the workplaces can pose some risks in the efficiency and the productivity.

Digital communication means and organizational flexibilities enable home office and distant working. Although distant and flexible working allow employees work whenever and wherever they want. Employees can benefit from this flexibility. Because they do not have to be present physically in the workplace or be stick to any time schedule such as 08:00–17:00 daily working hours. So, employees can freely plan daily activities and allocate enough time for the private life and socialization or family issues. However, technologies which enable flexible and distant working certainly pose some risks for employees. The first and most important result of home office work is that the work-life balance of the employees can be disrupted. The boundaries between work and life disappear due to digitalization (Schwarzmüller et al., 2018, pp. 122–123). Depending on the personality and leadership style of the employees, there is the possibility of never-ending working hours. A hard-working employee works day and night to carry out tasks assigned by managers, and when tasks are fulfilled, a new one comes. After a while this cycle becomes a frustrating process for the employee, and time for private and social life is completely lost. Leaders must consider this risk as the part of the health management issues.

On the other hand, digital communication means generate massive information by e-mails, social media feeds or instant messaging groups. The information overload is another challenge for employees to struggle not to get distracted (Schwarzmüller et al., 2018, p. 124).

Virtual teams are commonly composed of physically dispersed team members. Similarly, distant working, home office, and flexible working applications, enabled by digital communication technologies, facilitate traditional co-located team members operate in the physically dispersed locations. This new situation, which is one of the consequences of digital transformation, provide some advantages to organization in terms of aligning organization structure and working style to contemporary needs of business and community. Despite these advantages, it brings some challenges such as disappearance of boundaries between private life and work life, change in organizational structure and business processes, and difficulties in communication and coordination compared to face-to-face and co-located traditional workplaces.

Digital workplace environment may cause occupational some diseases such as repetitive stress injury (RSI), carpal tunnel syndrome (CTS), computer vision syndrome (CVS) (Laudon & Laudon, 2018, pp. 180–183), work posture, musculoskeletal system disorders and low back pain (Küçük et al., 2018, p. 136).

RSI occurs due to the prolonged repetitive, vigorous or awkward hand movements and is often seen in tennis players. The digital workforce is at risk from overuse of the hands and wrist to perform a repetitive task such as typing on the keypad and clicking the mouse. The consequences can be very serious and cause annoying pain and even disability (Kayode et al., 2015, p. 1). CTS is common type of repetitive stress injuries. CTS causes numbness, tingling, burning sensation or pain in the hand. CTS can seriously disrupt precise clamping, manual adjustment and computer usage in work and daily activities, resulting in reduced productivity (Roquelaure et al., 2020, p. 2). Low back pain (LBP) is common among digital workforce and is the most common reason of work-related disability in employee under 45. Although there are many causes, there are studies significantly showing that poor workplace ergonomics is the primary cause of back pain (Janwantanakul et al., 2011, p. 1). Workplace design and intensive computer usage cause musculoskeletal disorders as well (Estember & Aguila, 2020, p. 325). CVS is a major health risk for digital workplaces. Because every digital device has a screen and visual output features. The American Optometric Association defines CVS as problems with the eyes and vision caused by prolonged computer use. The most common symptoms associated with CVS are eye strain, blurred vision, dry eyes, and headaches (Artime Ríos et al., 2020, p. 1240).

Due to mentioned health risks, measures should be taken to protect digital workforce in the workplaces. Workstations should be designed according to the natural wrist position. Using wrist support pads to support the wrist, appropriate computer desks, ergonomic keyboards and underfoot supports can prevent posture disorders and reduce repetitive stress injuries. Some managerial and processual measures can be taken such as well scheduled rest breaks, rotation plan to change job among employees (Laudon & Laudon, 2018, p. 180).

One of the problems posed by digital workplaces (computers, Internet, digital communication means, mobile devices, virtual technology etc.) is threat to mental and cognitive abilities. Computer make it easier for us to calculate any mathematical transaction. But we use computer or mobile phones even for quite simple transactions such as addition or multiplication of one-digit numbers. Today enterprise resource planning software are combining all functions in the organization and generating reports, decisions and any information which managers need. Similarly, Internet promptly show us whatever we need, eventually we are getting addiction. As the all other addiction this digital addiction has the potential of danger for us. If some brain areas and functions are not used, these areas become blind and lose their abilities (Loh & Kanai, 2016, pp. 1–11; Maurer, 2015, p. 49; Moledina & Khoja, 2018, p. 12; Sparrow et al., 2011, p. 776). Especially the new generation, who has been exposed to digital technology all their lives, will be the human resources of companies in the near future. Therefore, managers need to be interested in digital dementia research, which has emerged as a new research area and focuses on the impact of computers and the Internet on human cognition.

6.8 Conclusion

As a result, it is inevitable that technology develops and this development transforms society, industry, in short, all aspects of life. A new and disruptive technology emerge almost every day. Today, we experience that every product, service, even workplaces, working styles are transformed by digitalization. This transformation continues at a dizzying pace, and organizations and individuals have hardly any chance of staying out of these changes. Although the need for transformation is sometimes necessary, it generally happens voluntarily because of the benefits it promises. Organizations and companies can perform global operations by digitizing their management and business functions, fast and high-quality production, effective customer relationship management, and cooperation with any company in the world. They can get all benefits at a lower cost than traditional methods.

However, despite these benefits, digital transformation brings some problems and risks. It transforms the organizational structure and description and causes the emergence of virtual organizations and networks with digital communication means. These developments bring difficulties in communication, coordination and management processes. Geographically dispersed business units or distant working make coordination difficult. On the other hand, digital communication means and being available at anytime and anywhere disturb work-life balance. Furthermore, AI robots become autonomies teammates that is completely weird and change dramatically working places. The aspects of digital workplaces and working environments that threaten the health of employees have also started to emerge. Digital workforce occupational diseases include social isolation, stress due to increasing job demand, repetitive stress injuries, CTS, CVS, work posture problems, musculoskeletal system disorders and low back pain. As the digitalization level of the business increases, it brings problems such as technology dependency and vulnerability against cyberattacks. A sudden and unexpected cyberattack can collapse a global operation. The image and brand value of the company can be damaged and serious financial losses occur. Even if everything goes well, the digital transformation brings a huge investment cost and can change the business description of firm or the sector in which it belongs.

Today, managing this transformation and change successfully is the most fundamental challenge of managers. To achieve this, firstly managers must be aware of change and develop personal and organizational digital literacy. Secondly managers should consider dark side of adaption of any technology. In addition, emerging technologies, with transformative power, should be monitored and recognized by a team of experts and managers. Early phase of a new transformation noticed by company could offer unique opportunities.

References

Albach, H., Meffert, H., Pinkwart, A., & Reichwald, R. (2015). Management of Permanent Change – New Challenges and Opportunities for Change Management. In H. Albach, H. Meffert, A. Pinkwart, & R. Reichwald (Eds.), *Management of Permanent Change*. Springer.

Armaou, M., Konstantinidis, S., & Blake, H. (2020). The effectiveness of digital interventions for psychological well-being in the workplace: A systematic review protocol. *International Journal of Environmental Research and Public Health*, *17*(1). https://doi.org/10.3390/ijerph17010255

Artime Ríos, E. M., Suárez Sánchez, A., Sánchez Lasheras, F., & Seguí Crespo, M. del M. (2020). Genetic algorithm based on support vector machines for computer vision syndrome classification in health personnel. *Neural Computing and Applications*, *32*(5), 1239–1248. https://doi.org/10.1007/s00521-018-3581-3.

Banks, G. C., Dionne, S. D., Sayama, H., Schmid, M., & Special, M. (2019). Leadership in the digital era: Social media, big data, virtual reality, computational methods, and deep learning. *The Leadership Quarterly*, *30*(5), 101325. https://doi.org/10.1016/s1048-9843(19)30520-x.

Baptista, J., Stein, M. K., Klein, S., Watson-Manheim, M. B., & Lee, J. (2020). Digital work and organisational transformation: Emergent Digital/Human work configurations in modern organisations. *Journal of Strategic Information Systems*, *29*(2), 101618. https://doi.org/10.1016/j.jsis.2020.101618

Bondar, S., Hsu, J. C., Pfouga, A., & Stjepandić, J. (2017). Agile digital transformation of System-of-Systems architecture models using Zachman framework. *Journal of Industrial Information Integration*, *7*(April), 33–43. https://doi.org/10.1016/j.jii.2017.03.001.

Ceruzzi, P. E. (2013). *A History of Modern Computing*. MIT Press. https://doi.org/10.1017/CBO9781107415324.004.

Chakraborti, T., Kambhampati, S., Scheutz, M., & Zhang, Y. (2017). *AI Challenges in Human-Robot Cognitive Teaming*. ArXiv. http://arxiv.org/abs/1707.04775.

Charlier, S. D., Stewart, G. L., Greco, L. M., & Reeves, C. J. (2016). Emergent leadership in virtual teams: A multilevel investigation of individual communication and team dispersion antecedents. *Leadership Quarterly*, *27*(5), 745–764. https://doi.org/10.1016/j.leaqua.2016.05.002.

Cortellazzo, L., Bruni, E., & Zampieri, R. (2019). The role of leadership in a digitalized world: A review. *Frontiers in Psychology*, *10*(AUG), 1–21. https://doi.org/10.3389/fpsyg.2019.01938.

Drucker, P. F. (2012). *Management: Tasks, Responsibilities, Practices*. Taylor & Francis Group.

Eilon, S. (2012). *Management Strategies: A Critique of Theories And Practices*. Springer.

Estember, R. D., & Aguila, D. K. S. (2020). The Effects of the Workplace Design, Work Methods Design and Health Problems and Occupational Diseases in the Prevalence of Musculoskeletal Disorders among Bank Tellers. *2020 IEEE 7th International Conference on Industrial Engineering and Applications, ICIEA 2020*, 321–325. https://doi.org/10.1109/ICIEA49774.2020.9101974.

Gimple, H., Huber, R. X. R., Roglinger, M., Hosseini, S., Probst, L., & Faisst, U. (2018). Structuring digital transformation: A framework of action fields and its application at ZEISS. *Journal of Information Technology Theory and Application*, *19*(1), 31–54. https://doi.org/10.1111/j.1467-8276.2007.00999.x.

Gobble, M. A. M. (2018). Digitalization, digitization, and innovation. *Research Technology Management*, *61*(4), 56–59. https://doi.org/10.1080/08956308.2018.1471280.

Gombolay, M. C., Gutierrez, R. A., Clarke, S. G., Sturla, G. F., & Shah, J. A. (2015). Decision-making authority, team efficiency and human worker satisfaction in mixed human–robot teams. *Autonomous Robots*, *39*(3), 293–312. https://doi.org/10.1007/s10514-015-9457-9.

Griffin, R. W. (2012). *Management*. Cancage Learning.

Hirt, M., & Willmott, P. (2014). Strategic principles for competing in the digital age. *McKinsey Quarterly*, *5*(1), 1–13. https://doi.org/10.1007/s13398-014-0173-7.2.

IBM Security. (2020). *Cost of Data Breach Report 2020 (Highlights)*. https://www.ibm.com/security/digital-assets/cost-data-breach-report/#/.

Issa, A., Hatiboglu, B., Bildstein, A., & Bauernhansl, T. (2018). Industrie 4.0 roadmap: Framework for digital transformation based on the concepts of capability maturity and alignment. *Procedia CIRP*, *72*, 973–978. https://doi.org/10.1016/j.procir.2018.03.151.

Janwantanakul, P., Pensri, P., Moolkay, P., & Jiamjarasrangsi, W. (2011). Development of a risk score for low back pain in office workers – a cross-sectional study. *BMC Musculoskeletal Disorders*, *12*(1), 23. https://doi.org/10.1186/1471-2474-12-23.

Johnson, C. E., & Hackman, M. Z. (2018). *Leadership: A Communication Perspective.* Waveland Press.

Jung, M. F., Lee, J. J., Depalma, N., Adalgeirsson, S. O., Hinds, P. J., & Breazeal, C. (2013). Engaging robots: Easing complex human-robot teamwork using backchanneling. *Proceedings of the ACM Conference on Computer Supported Cooperative Work, CSCW*, 1555–1566. https://doi.org/10.1145/2441776.2441954.

Kagerman, H. (2015). Change Through Digitization – Value Creation in the Age of Industry 4.0. In H. Albach, H. Meffert, A. Pinkwart, & R. Reichwald (Eds.), *Management of Permanent Change* (pp. 23–45). Springer. https://doi.org/10.1007/978-3-658-05014-6_1.

Kayode, A. A., Adewale, J. A., & Lawal, N. T. A. (2015). An exploration of prevalence of repetitive stress injuries among computer operators in Nigeria. *International Journal of Computer Applications*, *109*(1), 1–5. https://doi.org/10.5120/19149-0568.

Klassen, A. (2019). Deconstructing paper-lined cubicles: Digital literacy and information technology resources in the workplace. *International Journal of Advanced Corporate Learning (IJAC)*, *12*(3), 5. https://doi.org/10.3991/ijac.v12i3.11170.

Kohnke, O. (2017). It's Not Just About Technology: The People Side of Digitization. In G. Oswald & M. Kleinemeier (Eds.), *Shaping the Digital Enterprise: Trends and Use Cases in Digital Innovation and Transformation* (pp. 1–335). Springer International Publishing. https://doi.org/10.1007/978-3-319-40967-2.

Küçük, F., Düzenli Öztürk, S., Şenol, H., & Özkeskin, M. (2018). Ofis Çalışanlarında Çalışma Postürü, Kas İskelet Sistemi Rahatsızlıkları, Bel Ağrısına Bağlı Özürlülük Düzeyi ve Sağlıkla İlgili Yaşam Kalitesinin İncelenmesi. *Ergoterapi ve Rehabilitasyon Dergisi*, *6*(2), 135–144. https://doi.org/10.30720/ered.463658.

Larson, L., & DeChurch, L. A. (2020). Leading teams in the digital age: Four perspectives on technology and what they mean for leading teams. *Leadership Quarterly*, *31*(1), 1–18. https://doi.org/10.1016/j.leaqua.2019.101377.

Laudon, K. C., & Laudon, J. P. (2018). *Management Information Systems Managing the Digital Firm* (15th ed.). Pearson Education Limited.

Legner, C., Eymann, T., Hess, T., Matt, C., Böhmann, T., Drews, P., Mädche, A., Urbach, N., & Ahlemann, F. (2017). Digitalization: Opportunity and challenge for the business and information systems engineering community. *Business and Information Systems Engineering, 59*(4), 301–308. https://doi.org/10.1007/s12599-017-0484-2.

Li, F. (2020). The digital transformation of business models in the creative industries: A holistic framework and emerging trends. *Technovation, 92–93*(November), 1–10. https://doi.org/10.1016/j.technovation.2017.12.004.

Loh, K. K., & Kanai, R. (2016). How has the Internet reshaped human cognition? *Neuroscientist, 22*(5), 506–520. https://doi.org/10.1177/1073858415595005.

Luo, P., Ng-Thow-Hing, V., & Neff, M. (2013). An Examination of Whether People Prefer Agents Whose Gestures Mimic Their Own. In R. Aylett (Ed.), *ILecture Notes in Computer Science (including subseries Lecture Notes in Artificial Intelligence and Lecture Notes in Bioinformatics) Vol. 8108 LNAI.* (pp. 229–238). Springer Berlin Heidelberg. https://doi.org/10.1007/978-3-642-40415-3_20.

Lynch, R. (2015). *Strategic Management Seventh Edition*. Pearson.

Malatji, M., Marnewick, A., & von Solms, S. (2020). Validation of a socio-technical management process for optimising cybersecurity practices. *Computers and Security, 95*(1), 101846. https://doi.org/10.1016/j.cose.2020.101846.

Matt, C., Hess, T., & Benlian, A. (2015). Digital transformation strategies. *Business and Information Systems Engineering, 57*(5), 339–343. https://doi.org/10.1007/s12599-015-0401-5.

Maurer, H. (2015). Does the Internet make us stupid? *Communications of the ACM, 58*(1), 48–51. https://doi.org/10.1145/2629544.

Moledina, S., & Khoja, A. (2018). Digital dementia – is smart technology making us dumb? *Ochsner Journal, 18*(1), 12. https://doi.org/10.1043/1524-5012-18.1.12.

Morris, D., Madzudzo, G., & Garcia-Perez, A. (2020). Cybersecurity threats in the auto industry: Tensions in the knowledge environment. *Technological Forecasting and Social Change, 157*(May), 1–8 (120102). https://doi.org/10.1016/j.techfore.2020.120102.

Nahavandi, A. (2014). *The Art and Science of Leadership*. Pearson.

Oswald, G., & Kleinemeier, M. (2017). Shaping the Digital Enterprise: Trends and Use Cases in Digital Innovation and Transformation. In *Shaping the Digital Enterprise: Trends and Use Cases in Digital Innovation and Transformation* (pp. 1–339). Springer International Publishing. https://doi.org/10.1007/978-3-319-40967-2_13.

Pfeffermann, N. (2019). *New Leadership in Strategy and Communication*. Springer.

Pryor, M. G., Humphreys, J., Taneja, S., & Toombs, L. (2011). Where are the new organization theories? Evolution, development and theoretical debate. *International Journal of Management, 28*(3), 959.

Rahman, M. H. (2012). Henry Fayol and Frederick Winslow Taylor's contribution to management thought: An overview. *ABC Journal of Advanced Research, 1*(2), 94–103. https://doi.org/10.18034/abcjar.v1i2.10.

Robbins, S. P., & Coulter, M. (2012). *Management*. Pearson Education. Inc., publishing as Prentice Hall.

Robbins, S. P., & Judge, T. A. (2017). *Organizational Behavior, Global Edition*. Pearson Education Limited.

Robbins, S. P., Decenzo, D. A., & Coulter, M. (2014). *Fundamentals of Management: Essentials Concepts and Applications (Global Edition)*. Pearson Education Limited.

Roquelaure, Y., Garlantézec, R., Rousseau, V., Descatha, A., Evanoff, B., Mattioli, S., Goldberg, M., Zins, M., & Bodin, J. (2020). Carpal tunnel syndrome and exposure to work-related biomechanical stressors and chemicals: Findings from the Constances cohort. *PLoS ONE, 15*(6 June), 1–17. https://doi.org/10.1371/journal.pone.0235051.

Sauppé, A., & Mutlu, B. (2014). Robot Deictics: How Gesture and Context Shape Referential Communication. *9th ACM/IEEE International Conference on Human-Robot Interaction (HRI)*, 342–349.

Schmidt, C., Praeg, C. P., & Gunther, J. (2018). Designing Digital Workplace Environments. *2018 IEEE International Conference on Engineering, Technology and Innovation, ICE/ITMC 2018 – Proceedings*. https://doi.org/10.1109/ICE.2018.8436349.

Schwarzmüller, T., Brosi, P., Duman, D., & Welpe, I. M. (2018). How does the digital transformation affect organizations? Key themes of change in work design and leadership. *Management Revue, 29*(2), 114–138. https://doi.org/10.5771/0935-9915-2018-2-114.

Sener, E., & Yuksel, A. N. (2017). The reflections of digitalization at organizational level: industry 4.0 in Turkey. *Journal of Business, Economics and Finance, 6*(3), 291–300. https://doi.org/10.17261/pressacademia.2017.688.

Sparrow, B., Liu, J., & Wegner, D. M. (2011). Google effects on memory: Cognitive consequences of having information at our fingertips. *Science, 333*(6043), 776–778. https://doi.org/10.1126/science.1207745.

Valentine, E., & Stewart, G. (2015). Enterprise business technology governance: Three competencies to build board digital leadership capability. *Proceedings of the Annual Hawaii International Conference on System Sciences, 48th*, 4513–4522. https://doi.org/10.1109/HICSS.2015.539.

Vial, G. (2019). Understanding digital transformation: A review and a research agenda. *Journal of Strategic Information Systems, 28*(2), 118–144. https://doi.org/10.1016/j.jsis.2019.01.003.

Yoo, Y., Henfridsson, O., & Lyytinen, K. (2010). The new organizing logic of digital innovation: An agenda for information systems research. *Information Systems Research, 21*(4), 724–735. https://doi.org/10.1287/isre.1100.0322.

Yoo, Y., Jr, R. J. B., Lyytinen, K., & Majchrzak, A. (2012). *Yoo et al. 23*(5), 1398–1408.

Yukl, G. (2008). *Leadership in Organizations, Seventh Edition*. Pearson Prentice Hall.

Zeki, C. P. (2009). The importance of non-verbal communication in classroom management. *Procedia – Social and Behavioral Sciences, 1*(1), 1443–1449. https://doi.org/10.1016/j.sbspro.2009.01.254.

Mehmet Sıtkı Saygılı

7. LOGISTICS OPERATION CHALLENGES OF DIGITAL ORGANIZATIONS

Abstract In recent years, traditional business processes of companies have been digitalized due to the digital transformation in world trade, intense competition conditions and changing customer expectations. Companies transform into digital organizations by adapting their business culture, employees, infrastructure, activities and operations to this transformation. In this context, third-party logistics service providers, which are among the main components of the supply chain, do not remain indifferent to this process and invest in digitalization in order to meet the scope of services demanded by digital organizations. The digitalization of logistics processes provides companies with instant and simple communication, fast and low-error operations, and thus, operating costs of companies are reduced. However, there are various difficulties that adversely affect logistics processes in the supply chain because of customs regulations and tariffs, legal regulations, natural disasters and epidemics, non-integrated business processes and delayed investments, cybersecurity threats, organizational culture and employee motivation. The subject of this study is to address the reasons for the challenges of digital organizations that they outsource the logistics services in the supply chain.

Keywords: *digitalization, logistics challenges, supply chain*

7.1 Digital Trade and Digital Organizations

International trade has entered a new phase with the developments in information communication technologies. In order for companies to stand out in the competition, they need to plan their business processes better than their competitors, make faster and more accurate decisions, and accelerate the management of processes by exchanging real-time information. The production and use of digital data leads to the digitalization of economies, trade and organizations. In the business world, digitalization means activating, improving and/or transforming business operations and/or business functions and/or business models/processes and/or activities by using digitalized data through digital technologies (Yankın, 2019: 12).

Developments in information communication technologies increase productivity in macroeconomic terms. For this reason, an economy needs to include new technologies, especially complex technologies that have an impact on the economy such as artificial intelligence, into its structure and use it effectively (Meltzer, 2019: 28). This leads to the digitalization of trade. While digital trade was previously perceived as the trade of goods and services using the internet, today it is a broad concept that includes innovations in the digital environment such as global value chains, services that enable smart production and the provision of free information flow (Burri & Polanco, 2020: 190). Although the data flow enables the trading transactions to be carried out digitally, not all digital trade transactions are delivered digitally. In this context, digital commerce includes both digital and physical delivered goods and services (González & Jouanjean, 2017: 13). The rapid development of the Internet and other information and communication technologies has led to an increase in the electronic cross-border distribution of services and digital products such as sound recordings, audiovisual works, video games, computer software and literary works (Sacha & Hold, 2012: 179). Digital processes are also used in the supply, production and distribution processes of physically delivered products.

Companies need to take full advantage of digital technologies to have a more effective organization and reach higher number of customers, regardless of the physicality of their products (Kane et al., 2016: 6). For this reason, companies evolve into digital organizations. Digital organizations are companies that have completed their transformation in the digital service and operational competence and have structured their corporate structures in a way that will have maximum benefit from new digital business models (Karaduman & Elgin, 2017: 5). Digitalization in trade reduces the marginal production and distribution costs not only for large companies but also for small companies, entrepreneurs and individuals. It increases access to global trade by promoting innovation in business models and by enabling the emergence of micro-multinational companies, jobs and supply chains that can take advantage of global opportunities (Lund, 2016: 1). The challenge here to be overcome is to ensure the highest possible level and uninterrupted data visibility, accuracy, and consistency of data flow with real-time continuity of the operation.

7.2 Logistics Activities in Digital Organizations

Logistics services cover transportation, distribution, material handling, storage, customs clearance, packaging and insurance business processes. Logistics management consists of activities that include strategic, operational and tactical planning of inbound and outbound logistics processes that flow of all kinds of products, services and information about them from the starting point to the consumption point or vice versa (CSCMP, 2013). Third-party services offered by the logistics industry enable companies to gain service and cost advantages in business processes that fall within the scope of logistics activities (Lai et al., 2005: 1). The quality of the provided logistics service plays an important role in the company's competitiveness. In digital trade, logistics services positively affect access of companies to the market, growth, export and sales figures, while also positively affect costs of consumers to find more options to meet their needs, and delivery times (Huria, 2019: 13). The digitalization of commercial activities has also led to the digitalization of logistics services, which are also a part of trade. The use of new technologies in logistics processes enables information to be collectively obtained, processed, stored, analyzed, visualized, transmitted and shared at a very low cost (Estrada et al., 2019: 3). The internationalization of companies depends on having reliable, easy-to-use logistics systems with global reach. It is thought that digitally developed cross-border logistics services will increase the commercial activities of companies, especially small and medium sized enterprises (SME), worldwide (World Economic Forum, 2016: 15).

Presence of smart devices and utilization of applications such as intelligent distributed control systems, various management and control solutions, Internet of Things (IoT), automatic identification systems, network communication systems, GPS tracking systems, cyber-physical systems (CPS), standardized data communication networks, web-based cloud solutions etc. further contributes to the real-time management of large amounts of information and operational efficiency in the logistics industry. At the same time, the use of these practices significantly affects the functioning of the economy, the labor market and the competition conditions (Illés et al., 2018: 220). In spite of all these positive aspects, various challenges arise in logistics service processes and they negatively affect digital organizations in the supply chain.

7.3 Digital Organizations and Logistics Operations Challenges

Companies face various potential risks due to outsourcing services. These risks are the loss of knowledge, skills, control and flexibility in their activities, deteriorating business relationships, poor performance, loss of reputation (Villani & Greco, 2018: 108), and as a result, increase in costs and vulnerability in competition. Digital organizations are also exposed to these risks due to the logistics services they outsource. The main reason for this is that there are various challenges in the logistics service process due to customs procedures and tariffs, legal regulations, natural disasters and epidemics, non-integrated business processes and delayed investments, cybersecurity threats, organizational culture and employee motivation.

7.4 Customs Procedures and Tariffs

Countries work in order to harmonize customs regulations and modernize customs business processes. Especially in international trade, the trade costs incurred regarding customs and other border controls are an important issue for companies. Business people may not be fully aware of customs regulations such as taxes, documents and processing times (Pratamasari, 2020: 5), and simply, for many businesses it is important to know clearly the documents required and the customs duties and fees to be paid on cross-border shipments (World Economic Forum, 2018: 11). Logistics service providers follow the procedures regarding these regulations in import and export processes. In addition, logistics companies and customs brokers constitute one party of the business processes that need to be followed regarding customs procedures, while the other party is the customs authorities of the countries. In this context, the transactions made by both parties have an effect on whether there is an interruption in the customs clearance service to be provided to digital organizations.

Setting up a global logistics network and its ability to operate without any disruption is fraught with difficulties. In terms of customs clearance, complex customs regulations, constantly changing trade agreements and service disruptions caused by political factors in business processes put global logistics management in a difficult situation (Levans, 2019: 7). Due to the length of waiting duration caused by the density in customs, difficulties in transactions related to transit loads, declaration of goods and warehouse processes, and possible manmade errors, there may be disruptions in third-party logistics services and additional costs arise.

Today, another issue is the transformation of customs gates into customs walls as a result of the negative effects of trade wars. In global trade driven by digital technologies, trade based on global supply chains that benefit from cheap labor has been slowing down; whereas new digital technologies show that more actors than ever before can participate in cross-border transactions, from small businesses to multinational corporations. It is believed that this new era will lead to economic and social benefits, increase innovation and productivity, provide people with unprecedented access to knowledge and connect consumers and suppliers around the world (Lund & Tyson, 2018: 130). However, trade wars, which narrow the volume of foreign trade, appear as a barrier to logistics services in customs. A trade war is retaliation of a country by raising tariffs or imposing other trade barriers in response to trade barriers created by the counterparty (Köse & Ay, 2020: 122). A country that wants to retaliate against the other party can decline the products which are exported by the counterparty from the customs gates by making new requests, even though the products exported are presented to the customs by the logistics service provider in accordance with all procedures. Retaliation tariffs are detrimental to the welfare of countries that retaliate against each other (Breus, 2004: 257), although world trade is now under the influence of trade wars. The introverted policies of the states, especially the United States of America (USA), and the exit negotiations between the United Kingdom (UK) and the European Union (EU) negatively affect customs regulations of the countries, bureaucracy and ultimately logistics services in international trade. Companies that accept China as their production base and set up their global supply chain configuration accordingly may have to redesign their supply chains. On the other hand, although the conditions are not clear at the moment, the exit of the UK from the EU will make UK a third country in the EU. In this case, logistics companies that benefit from EU membership privileges while trading with the UK will have to keep up with the new rules. There may be new implementations for trade partners both in EU countries and in countries outside of the EU in matters such as customs procedures, customs duties, and import export declarations with the UK. According to the "Global Trade Report" of 2019, which shows the increase in protectionist measures in international trade, the protectionist measures of countries have increased in the last year and it has been a year in which more than a thousand protective measures have been put into effect, which have cumulatively affected 40 % of global trade negatively. In the report, it is stated that this development is not limited to the trade restriction measures introduced by the USA and China and has turned into a more general practice (Aran, 2020: 2). In this case, no matter how much companies invest in digitalization, they will not be able to prevent the disruptions in business processes and the increase in costs due to the shrinkage of trade and the disruption of logistics services as a result of changes in the customs policies of the countries.

7.5 Legal Challenges

As the opportunities offered by digital technologies increase, governments and regulators try to both preserve the integrity of their internal regulations and determine how they will benefit from the transition to digital. Ownership, access, collection, storage, use and dissemination of information require rules and policies (Andersson & Rosenqvist, 2018: 33) and as a result of more and more data going across borders for various purposes, and of increasing digitalization, it becomes important to address privacy and security issues without restrictive impact on trade. However, new business practices are not yet fully included in legal regulations that have lagged behind developments. Considering the current state of information communication technologies and the legal regulation regarding this phenomenon, it seems that there are gaps to be filled (Polanski & Johnston, 2002: 1). The digitalization process of trade legally has still gray areas. For example, many countries, including the USA, are currently lack of regulations or laws that recognize electronic securities rather than their written equivalents (Hoffman, 2019).

Production and logistics chains can be highly complex, whether between multinational companies, suppliers and customers. Electronic documentation using Machine to Machine (M2M) telemetry is used to expand logistics providers' ability to trace their goods on their international journey. For example, a container containing machine parts can be tracked from the factory to the port, traveling by sea, entering the destination country, and then delivered to the customer. Cross-border data flows reduce production costs and waste by providing more efficient and secure logistics process tracking (Wickham Heath Consulting, 2018: 18). However, there are various restrictions in the data flow of companies due to legal reasons. These restrictions include measures that do not allow data to be transferred across national borders, or measures that allow cross-border transfers but require a copy of data to be kept domestically, and the requirement to obtain prior permission to transfer data abroad. Countries may request the data to be localized in order to protect personal data or to ensure cybersecurity (Meltzer, 2020). Countries that require M2M data to be managed by national servers limit the country's ability to participate in the global economy (Wickham Heath Consulting, 2018: 18). Restrictions arising from legal regulations adversely affect digital supply chains.

7.6 Natural Disasters and Epidemics

Natural disasters and epidemics negatively affect the supply chain of digital organizations and the logistics services they receive in many ways. In such periods, safety stocks of companies decrease and delivery times increase. Natural disasters such as earthquakes and tsunamis in the world and infectious disease outbreaks such as the new corona virus (COVID-19) present global challenges for economic activities such as production operations, supply chain and logistics services (Singh et al., 2020: 1).

As a result of natural disasters, in logistics operations, distribution plans may be disrupted, transportation charges and durations may increase, deliveries may be delayed, fuel costs may increase and communication may be interrupted due to infrastructure damage. After the hurricane Tasha that hit Australia at the end of 2010, transportation routes were disrupted and the supply chain was adversely affected due to the disruption of storage and production facilities (Wisetjindawat et al., 2017: 1199). The Tohoku earthquake and tsunami that took place in 2011 resulted in a cost of $210 billion for Japan and affected supply chains worldwide. Unable to send or receive the necessary parts, Toyota G.M. and Nissan has temporarily closed its facilities in both the US and Japan. Similarly, when Hurricane Maria hit Puerto Rico in September 2017, the supply chains of the island's two largest industries, the pharmaceutical and medical devices industries, were destroyed (Carey, 2020). The interruption of the transportation infrastructure due to natural disasters causes the transportation and distribution activities included in the logistics services to be unable to be carried out, which means that companies cannot fully use their current production capacities. A company that is often forced to cease production due to the shortage of inputs caused by transportation disruptions will operate below its full capacity. The efficiency of the company will decrease due to less resource input and less output (Rozenberg et al., 2019: 12).

Another situation that disrupts supply chains and logistics services digital organizations is epidemics. Despite the numerous supply chain complications caused by disasters in the past decade, most companies today have been unprepared for the COVID-19 outbreak (Choi et al., 2020). A typical disruption in the supply chain has a geographical and/or industrial range. Also, the magnitude of the effect usually gets smaller as it gets further away from the center. An example is a hurricane that adversely affects business activities in a particular region. However, in the pandemic conditions that emerged with the COVID-19 outbreak, the whole world and all sectors are affected (Craighead et al., 2020: 839). Many logistics service providers face the challenge of bringing staff back at the beginning of the epidemic as they have reduced staffing numbers and switched to flexible working hours. As countries reopen their economies, shipping volumes increase due to increased demand, but delivery delays, congestion and higher freight rates are expected as distribution networks are blocked due to lack of capacity of carriers (Twinn et al., 2020: 5). All of these show the compelling effects of natural disasters and epidemic periods on supply chain and logistics services.

7.7 Non-Integrated Business Processes and Delayed Investments

In order to manage logistics services more efficiently, it is necessary to share complete, accurate and real-time data with all parties of the supply chain. In order to achieve this, companies in the logistics sector must use digital technologies. However, digital business processes have a wide ecosystem problem that requires new forms of digital collaboration, processes and infrastructure (Bharadwaj et al., 2013: 2). In the Doha tour negotiations, which were initiated in 2000 to increase liberalization and transparency in service trade, it was stated that there was a lack of access to technological distribution channels and information networks in the logistics sector (Burri, 2015: 37). Today, there are various challenges regarding data sharing in the logistics industry on the way to digitalization. These difficulties, which also affect other stakeholders of the chain, can be grouped as follows;

- Challenges arising from the integration of digital and physical business processes
- Challenges arising from investments
  - Challenges arising from technology investments
  - Challenges arising from infrastructure investments of the country

The first of the challenges arising from the integration of digital and physical business processes is that existing data is incomplete and inaccurate due to ongoing manual documentation or transfer of data by numerous people. The other is that it cannot be presented in a short time or is not presented to other process participants (Heistermann et al., 2016: 9). Many companies with small or large business volumes can be given as examples of this situation. For example, scanning of an incorrect barcode in the logistics service process may cause incorrect loading (Roth et al., 2013: 900). A cargo that is distributed can still appear at the transfer center because its status information is not updated in the system or is not processed into the system where it is embezzled by the delivery courier. In this case, you may not be at the address because of lack of knowledge that your cargo will be arriving today, but your cargo will be delivered precisely on that day. There are also companies that close themselves to the transfer of information and do not want to share their data. Logistics companies that cannot fully fill their trucks carry the excess demand loads of other logistics companies to fill their free space. However, these companies, which go to such a business partnership, do not integrate their information systems together because they are worried about the exposure of their customer portfolios. Information is shared not in real time, but by being transferred from one company to another through its employees.

Failure of the logistics companies or other companies in the supply chain to make the necessary investments creates difficulties in operation management. For example, the assessment made in terms of the use of digital technologies in Turkey, the applications they use in supply chain and logistics processes of the company is seen as insufficient (T.C. Sanayi ve Teknoloji Bakanlığı, 2018: 91). In logistics services, the potential of digitalization cannot be fully exploited and cannot be utilized to obtain optimum benefit. Although a common platform is created where all parties share the necessary information in the logistics service process consisting of independent parties such as transport brokers, third-party logistics service providers, and carriers, this cannot be operated efficiently (Gallay et al., 2017: 20). Similarly, existing global shipping platforms generally either consolidate small quantity shipments and deliver them to the dominant logistics service providers under a single account; or act as a price comparison engine between these service providers (World Economic Forum, 2016: 15). However, the available resources can be used more effectively to provide solutions for specific customer demands. International information and document records can be kept. Options about payment terms and conditions may be offered. Door-to-door tracking can be provided. Demand for partial loads can be combined. Alternative routes and modes of transport can be proposed with route optimization. In addition, lack of infrastructure investments leads to difficulties in information communication technologies. In order to ensure full digitalization and a sustainable success, not only individual companies or the sector, but also countries should invest in infrastructure for information communication technologies.

7.8 Cybersecurity Threats

Supply chains are part of a complex global system where data and information are shared through cyberspace. It is also a series of virtual organizations that form a network through which product, service, information and finance flow (Urciuoli et al., 2013: 53). The more links a supply chain has, the more vulnerable it becomes. This increases the importance of the safe processing and storage of data. The information transmitted in supply chains can become targets of cyberattacks (Ghadge et al., 2020: 224). The interconnectedness of companies makes them an attractive target for attackers aiming to launch cyberattacks. For this reason, it's of great importance for logistics companies to invest in ways to protect sensitive data and information.

Cybersecurity mainly deals with security issues in cyberspace. Cybersecurity is basically based on the protection of cyber space from all kinds of threats. It is a holistic and compiling concept. It is a unifying element that encompasses all layers from the smallest cybercrime to the largest and most complex attack (Bıçakcı, 2019: 1). The results of activities carried out in cyberspace can be physical and affect people with or without awareness (Ünal & Ergen, 2018: 192). Therefore, along with the security of information sources, cybersecurity also includes the protection of other assets, including the person himself/herself (Solms & Niekerk, 2013: 97).

The most common types of cyberattacks are Phishing, Malware, DoS and DDoS, Man in The Middle, SQL Injection, Zero Day Exploit, Passwords Attack, Eavesdropping Attack and Birthday Attack. The general scope of these types of attacks is described below (Bendovschi, 2015: 25; Marshall & Saulawa, 2015: 7; Seemma et al., 2018: 127).

- Phishing: Attacks aimed at stealing confidential information by treating people as a reliable source.
- Malware: Used by an attacker to compromise the privacy, availability, and integrity of data. Worms, viruses, trojans are examples of these, which are leaked into computer systems without people's permission.
- Dos and DDoS: Attacks where the attacker tries to prevent online services from working properly by filling the victim (e.g., the server) with commands. DDoS means carrying out these attacks from more than one computer.
- Man in the Middle: Cyberattacks that occur when an attacker intervenes between two communication ends. Every message sent from source A to source B reaches the attacker before reaching its destination, and every action taken can be seen by the attacker. The risks posed by this type of attack are the possibility of unauthorized access to sensitive information or the possibility of altering the information / message reaching the target by the attacker.
- SQL Injection: It is a type of cyberattack targeting databases. Attackers take control of victims' databases by exploiting SQL vulnerabilities.
- Zero Day Exploit: Zero-day vulnerabilities are software or hardware flaws that have not been detected before but will cause serious attacks and are difficult to detect until the attack occurs. Zero-day attack is when an attacker exploits vulnerability and spreads malware before developers have time to release a patch or fix.
- Passwords Attack: Attacks aimed at breaking passwords used while entering a system.

- Eavesdropping Attack: In this type of attack, attackers infiltrate a network and eavesdrop on personal data such as credit card information, passwords and conversations that users send over that network.
- Birthday Attack: The birthday attack is a type of cryptographic attack that uses the mathematics behind the birthday problem in probability theory. It is done against hashing algorithms used to verify the integrity of a message, software or digital signature.

In the supply chain management process, large amounts of data are shared through online networks between manufacturers, suppliers, contractors, shipping and trading companies (Burrell et al., 2020: 2). Logistics services are connected through corporate networks. Thus, information is integrated and shared between businesses. This helps companies remotely monitor and manage operations but also increases the likelihood of cyberattacks. When the system is connected to a large network, it can be accessed by malicious software (Sarder & Haschak, 2019: 1). Since the information systems of all members in the supply chain are interconnected, the most fundamental cyber risk in logistics and supply chain networks is the 'system risk' that the entire system is broken when a malfunction occurs in the information system (Cheung & Bell, 2019: 2). According to a study conducted by Cisco, transportation companies use much less cybersecurity tools compared to other industries. It is observed that the sector falls behind other sectors by 10 % to 20 % in using cybersecurity technologies, especially in areas such as e-mail and message security, mobile security, access control and authorization, identity management (UTİKAD, 2017).

It is an obligation to take the necessary precautions against cybersecurity risk in logistics services. In the international cyberattack organized with a ransomware called WannaCry in May 2017, logistics companies were also attacked by cyberattacks, along with other targets such as companies operating in the energy and health sector. Among the victims of this attack are TNT Express, a Dutch-based cargo shipping company, the French railway company SNCF, and Danish-based A.P. There is the Moller-Maersk Group. From each computer it attacked, the virus requested a ransom of $300–600 within three days in exchange for decrypting the files and disks it locked on infected computers (Koujalagi et al., 2018: 1). According to reports, a total of 300,000 systems were damaged in more than 150 countries due to the virus (Akbanov et al. 2019: 114). Also, in June 2017, another cyberattack, NotPetya took place. Maersk Line, Damco and APM Terminals, which are among the global companies of Maersk, were affected as a result of this attack. Delays and additional costs were incurred due to the ceasing operations of the company in the first days of the attack and then operating below its normal capacity. Later, extra costs were incurred in rebuilding IT. Regarding the Maersk group, 4,000 servers around the world, 45,000 computers were formatted and reinstalled; 2,500 applications were reinstalled (Eryaşa, 2020: 89). The network took 10 days to activate. During this period, export and import shipments of numerous companies around the world could not be made, and the customs procedures could not be initiated for container loads waiting at ports. It has been stated that Maersk company made a loss of approximately $300 million due to cyberattacks.

7.9 Organizational Culture and Employee Motivation

Organizational culture is the sum of values, norms, beliefs and philosophies that have the function of determining the way of doing business and behavior of the companies and that make each company unique and different from the others (Şeker & Bulduklu, 2018: 15). Organizational culture can sometimes prevent a new mindset from settling in a company. Cultural issues in digital transformation can become a bottleneck for companies. Even in the midst of a successful digital transformation, companies can see unions resisting. For example, in an airline company, flight employees adopt changes that enable business processes digitally, while ground employees who fear layoffs are extremely resistant in this process (MIT Center for Digital Business & Capgemini Consulting, 2017: 39). Logistics companies and their customers can show a performance-oriented development by using integrated logistics systems and information technologies (Karagöz & Akgün, 2015: 40). However, the lack of digital culture is seen as a major obstacle faced by the logistics sector (Barczak et al., 2019: 4) and makes it difficult to adapt to information technologies. There is a need for a cultural change that emphasizes teamwork and top management commitment to the changes that decentralized logistics operations will bring (nae, 2016).

Human beings are identified as both the biggest challenge and the main source of success for digital technologies. Employees have difficulty in changing their mindsets and beliefs, and they are stuck in their past success. However, success is achieved in digital technologies if cooperation can be made with employees (Cichosz et al., 2020: 212). For this reason, it is important to involve the human factor in the process. The common conclusion from studies examining the effect of digital transformation on employment management is that management of automations that ensure continuity with digital transformation will cause many complications and therefore the workforce needs to equip much more complex competencies (Gökalp et al., 2019: 206). Especially, the ability of employees in the logistics sector to collect, store and statistically analyze data in a structured way has become more and more important. For the workforce that needs to have complex competencies, the most classical problem in this transformation process is to give up habits. For this reason, it is seen that the employees resist this issue (Ünlü, 2020). Also, with digital transformation, businesses choose to work with digital freelancers who can work from anywhere. This situation causes the workforce to become globalized and exposed to higher competition (Foerster-Metz et al., 2018: 9). In this transformation, the motivation of employees who cannot meet their expectations in the company over time decreases and this situation has a negative impact on the business process (Ünsar et al., 2010: 251). To give an example, low employee motivation causes a decrease in productivity (Shaban et al., 2017: 1) and adversely affects company performance. The decrease in motivation also decreases the organizational commitment of the employee (Al-Madi et al., 2017: 134). The employee, whose organizational commitment is reduced, can engage in cyber loafing behavior in the digital environment (Niaei et al., 2014: 70). Cyber loafing occurs when information communication technologies offered to employees during working hours are used for individual purposes rather than for organizational purposes (Yıldız et al., 2015: 57). In addition, the use of personal mobile information communication technology devices by employees outside of corporate interests during working hours is also within the scope of cyber loafing behavior. Employees can engage in significant cyber loafing behaviors that are long term and pose potential risk of harm to the company and legal liability (Blanchard & Henle, 2008: 1068). For all these reasons, it is important that employees do not get scared from the digitalization process and continue their business processes without losing their motivation, so that the logistics services are not interrupted.

7.10 Conclusion

Recently, companies transform into organizations that carry their business processes to the digital world in order to save time, reduce costs and gain competitive advantage. Thus, speed, convenience, real-time data movement and storage, flexible mobility and new capabilities are gained by providing cooperation between departments and companies. Logistics service providers are also among the parties participating in this cooperation. With digitalization, all business plans related to supply chain and logistics management can be integrated with each other, supply chain visibility can be achieved, clearer analyzes for efficiency and process optimization are provided. However, bureaucracy and commercial obstacles arising from legal regulations in logistics business processes, regional and global restrictions due to disasters and epidemics, incomplete digitalization investments of the companies or countries that provide logistics services, disruptions in the integration of digital and physical business processes in data sharing, cyberattacks and inability of companies to fully adapt their institutional structures and employees to digitalization may cause deviations in planned business processes, and negatively affect their costs and competitive situations.

References

Akbanov, M., Vassilakis, V. G., & Logothetis, M. D. (2019). WannaCry Ransomware: Analysis of Infection, Persistence, Recovery Prevention and Propagation Mechanisms. *Journal of Telecommunications and Information Technology, 1*, 113–124.

Al-Madi, F. N., Assal, H., Shrafat, F., & Zeglat, D. (2017). The Impact of Employee Motivation on Organizational Commitment. *European Journal of Business and Management, 9*(15), 134–145.

Andersson, P., & Rosenqvist, C. (2018). Digitalization: Different Perspectives. In S. M. Per Andersson (Eds.), *Managing Digital Transformation.* Göteborg: SSE Institute for Research.

Aran, B. (2020). *2020 Yılında Ticaret Savaşları ve Beklentiler.* Türkiye Ekonomi Politikaları Araştırma Vakfı. Türkiye Ekonomi Politikaları Araştırma Vakfı (TEPAV).

Barczak, A., Izabela Dembińska, D., & Marzantowicz, Ł. (2019). Analysis of the Risk Impact of Implementing Digital Innovations for Logistics Management. *Processes, 7*(11), 1–16.

Bendovschi, A. (2015). Cyber-Attacks – Trends, Patterns and Security Countermeasures. *7th International Conference on Financial Criminology 2015. 28*, pp. 24–31. Oxford: Procedia Economics and Finance.

Bharadwaj, A., Sawy, O. A., Pavlou, P. A., & Venkatraman, N. (2013). Visions and Voices on Emerging Challenges in Digital Business Strategy. *MIS Quarterly, 37*(2), 1–30.

Bıçakcı, S. (2019, November). *Siber Güvenlik ve Savunma.* Accessed September 2020. Güvenlik Portalı: http://trguvenlikportali.com/wp-content/uploads/2019/11/SiberGuvenlik_SalihBicakci_v.1.pdf.

Blanchard, A. L., & Henle, C. A. (2008). Correlates of Different Forms of Cyberloafing: The Role of Norms and External Locus of Control. *Computers in Human Behavior, 24*(3), 1067–1084.

Breus, F. (2004). WTO Dispute Settlement: An Economic Analysis of Four EU–US Mini Trade Wars – A Survey. *Journal of Industry, Competition and Trade, 4*, 275–315.

Burrell, D. N., Bhargava, N., Bradley-Swanson, O., Harmon, M., Wright, J., Springs, D., & Dawson, M. (2020). Supply Chain and Logistics Management and an Open Door Policy Concerning Cybersecurity Introduction. *International Journal of Management and Sustainability, 9*(1), 1–10.

Burri, M. (2015). *The International Economic Law Framework for Digital Trade.* NCCR Trade Regulation Swiss National Centre of Competence in Research.

Burri, M., & Polanco, R. (2020). Digital Trade Provisions in Preferential Trade Agreements: Introducing a New Dataset. *Journal of International Economic Law, 23*, 187–220.

Carey, H. (2020, August 19). *The Impact of Natural Disasters on Economy and Supply Chain — and How to Prepare for the Worst.* Accessed September 2020. THOMAS: https://www.thomasnet.com/insights/how-natural-disasters-affect-the-supply-chain-and-how-to-prepare-for-the-worst/#register.

Cheung, K.-F., & Bell, M. G. (2019, in press). Attacker–Defender Model Against Quantal Response Adversaries for Cyber Security in Logistics Management: An Introductory Study. *European Journal of Operational Research* (https://doi.org/10.1016/j.ejor.2019.10.019), 1–11.

Choi, T. Y., Rogers, D., & Vakil, B. (2020, March 27). *Coronavirus Is a Wake-Up Call for Supply Chain Management.* Accessed September 2020. Harvard Business Review: https://hbr.org/2020/03/coronavirus-is-a-wake-up-call-for-supply-chain-management.

Cichosz, M., Wallenburg, C. M., & Knemeyer, A. M. (2020). Digital Transformation at Logistics Service Providers: Barriers, Success Factors and Leading Practices. *The International Journal of Logistics Management, 31*(2), 209–238.

Craighead, C. W., Jr., D. J., & Darby, J. L. (2020). Pandemics and Supply Chain Management Research: Toward a Theoretical Toolbox. *Decision Sciences, 51*(4), 838–866.

CSCMP. (2013). *CSCMP Supply Chain Management Definitions and Glossary.* Accessed September 2020: https://cscmp.org/CSCMP/Educate/SCM_Definitions_and_Glossary_of_Terms.aspx.

Eryaşa, E. (2020). Cyberspace Impacts on Maritime Sector. In H. N. Keleş, & A. E. (Eds.), *What's Happening in Cyber Space? An Interdisciplinary Approach.* Berlin: Peter Lang.

Estrada, M., Moliner, M.-Á., & Monferrer, D. (2019). The Digitalisation of Logistics. In W. D. (Eds.), *Advances in Business and Management: Volume 17.* Nova Science Publishers.

Foerster-Metz, U. S., Marquardt, K., Golowko, N., Kompalla, A., & Hell, C. (2018). Digital Transformation and Its Implications on Organizational Behavior. *Journal of EU Research in Business, 2018*(2018), 1–14.

Gallay, O., Korpela, K., Tapio, N., & Nurminen, J. K. (2017). A Peer-To-Peer Platform for Decentralized Logistics. *Proceedings of the Hamburg International Conference of Logistics (HICL) No.23* (pp. 19–34). Berlin: epubli GmbH.

Ghadge, A., Weiß, M., Caldwell, N. D., & Wilding, R. (2020). Managing Cyber Risk in Supply Chains: A Review and Research Agenda. *Supply Chain Management: An International Journal, 25*(2), 223–240.

Gökalp, E., Gökalp, M. O., Çoban, S., & Eren, P. E. (2019). Dijital Dönüşümün Etkisinde Verimli Istihdam Yönetimi: Yol Haritasi Önerisi. *Verimlilik Dergisi, 3*, 201–222.

González, J. L., & Jouanjean, M. A. (2017). *Digital Trade: Developing a Framework for Analysis.* OECD Trade Policy Papers, No. 205. Paris: OECD.

Heistermann, F., Mallée, T., & Hompel, M. T. (2016). *Digitisation in Logistics.* Bremen: BVL International.

Hoffman, C. (2019). *Regulatory and Legal Challenges around the Digitization of Trade and Shipping.* Accessed September 2020. Trade Finance Global: https://www.tradefinanceglobal.com/posts/regulatory-and-legal-challenges-around-the-digitization-of-trade-and-shipping/.

Huria, A. (2019). *Facilitating Trade and Logistics for E- Commerce Building Blocks, Challenges and Ways Forward.*Washington, DC: The World Bank/ World Bank Group.

Illés, B., Varga, A., & Czap, L. (2018). Logistics and Digitization. *Vehicle and Automotive Engineering 2 Proceedings of the 2nd VAE2018* (pp. 220–225). Miskolc: Springer.

Kane, G. C., Palmer, D., Phillips, A. N., Kiron, D., & Buckley, N. (2016). *Aligning the Organization for its Digital Future.* MIT Sloan Management Review and Deloitte University Press.

Karaduman, C., & Elgin, O. (2017). *Accenture Türkiye Dijitalleşme Endeksi 2016.* Accenture; Vodafone; Boğaziçi Üniversity; Middle East Technical University; Türkiye Bilişim Vakfı. Accenture.

Karagöz, İ. B., & Akgün, A. E. (2015). He Roles of It Capability and Organizational Culture on Logistics Capability and Firm Performance. *Journal of Business Studies Quarterly, 7*(2), 23–45.

Köse, Z., & Ay, M. K. (2020). Ticaret Savaşlarinin Lojistik Sektörüne Yansimasi. *R&S – Research Studies Anatolia Journal, 3*(2), 121–130.

Koujalagi, A., Patil, S., & Akkimaradi, P. (2018). The WannaCry Ransomeware, a Mega Cyber Attack and Their Consequences on the Modern India. *Engineering, 6*(4), 1–4.

Lai, K.-H., Ngai, E. W., & Cheng, T. C. (2005). Information Technology Adoption in Hong Kong's Logistics Industry. *Transportation Journal, 44*(4), 1–9.

Levans, M. (2019). *Global Logistics: Control what you can.* Accessed August 2020. Logistics Management: https://www.logisticsmgmt.com/article/global_logistics_control_what_you_can.

Lund, S. A. (2016). *How Digital Trade is Transforming Globalisation.* E15Initiative. Geneva: nternational Centre for Trade and Sustainable Development (ICTSD), World Economic Forum.

Lund, S., & Tyson, L. (2018). *Globalization Is Not in Retreat Digital Technology and the Future of Trade.* Accessed August 2020. Foreign Affairs: https://www.foreignaffairs.com/articles/world/2018-04-16/globalization-not-retreat.

Marshall, J. B., & Saulawa, M. A. (2015). Cyber-Attacks: The Legal Response. *International Journal of International Law, 1*(2), 1–18.

Meltzer, J. P. (2019). Governing Digital Trade. *World Trade Review, 18*(S1), 23–48.

Meltzer, J. P. (2020, March 06). *Data and the Transformation of International Trade.* Accessed August 2020. Brookings: https://www.brookings.edu/blog/up-front/2020/03/06/data-and-the-transformation-of-international-trade/.

MIT Center for Digital Business and Capgemini Consulting. (2017, 07). *Digital Transformation: A Roadmap for Billion-Dollar Organizations.* Accessed September 2020. Capgemini: https://www.google.com/search?client=safari&rls=en&q=DIGITAL+TRANSFORMATION:+A+ROADMAP+FOR+BILLION-DOLLAR+ORGANIZATIONS+FINDINGS+FROM+PHASE+1+OF+THE+DIGITAL+TRANSFORMATION+STUDY+CONDUCTED+BY+THE+MIT+CENTER+FOR+DIGITAL+BUSINESS+AND+CAPGEMINI+CONSULTING&ie=nae. (2016, August 26). *Digitalization Challenges in the Logistics Industry.* Accessed September 2020. nae global: https://nae.global/en/digitalization-challenges-in-the-logistics-industry/.

Niaei, M., Peidaei, M. M., & Nasiripour, A. A. (2014). The Relation Between Staff Cyberloafing and Organizational Commitment in Organization of Environmental Protection. *Kuwait Chapter of Arabian Journal of Business and Management Review, 3*(7), 59–71.

Polanski, P. P., & Johnston, R. B. (2002). Potential of Custom in Overcoming Legal Uncertainty in Global Electronic Commerce. *Journal of Information Technology Theory and Application, 4*(2), 1–16.

Pratamasari, A. (2020). Cybersecurity and Custom Regulations as Trade Barriers in ASEAN e-Commerce: Case of Indonesian e-Commerce. *Jurnal Global & Strategis, 14*(1), 1–16.

Roth, M., Klarmann, A., & Franczyk, B. (2013). Future Logistics – Challenges, Requirements and Solutions for Logistics Networks. *International Journal of Mechanical, Aerospace, Industrial, Mechatronic and Manufacturing Engineering, 7*(10), 898–903.

Rozenberg, J., Alegre, X. E., Avner, P., Fox, C., Hallegatte, S., Koks, E., . . . Tariverdi, M. (2019). *From a Rocky Road to Smooth Sailing: Building Transport Resilience to Natural Disasters.* Washington, DC: The World Bank.

Sacha, W.-V., & Hold, A. (2012). Towards Coherent Rules for Digital Trade: Building on Efforts in Multilateral Versus Preferential Trade Negotiations. In M. B. (Eds.), *Trade Governance in the Digital Age.* Cambridge, MA: Cambridge University Press.

Sarder, M., & Haschak, M. (2019, February). *Cyber Security and Its Implication on Material Handling and Logistics.* Accessed September 2020. MHI Solutions Community: https://www.mhi.org/downloads/industrygroups/solutions-community/white-papers/cyber-security.pdf.

Seemma, P. S., Nandhini, S., & Sowmiya, M. (2018). Overview of Cyber Security. *International Journal of Advanced Research in Computer and Communication Engineering, 7*(11), 125–128.

Shaban, O. S., Al-Zubi, Z., Ali, N., & Alqotaish, A. (2017). The Effect of Low Morale and Motivation on Employees' Productivity & Competitiveness in Jordanian Industrial Companies. *International Business Research, 10*(7), 1–7.

Singh, S., Kumar, R., Panchal, R., & Tiwari, M. K. (2020). Impact of COVID-19 on Logistics Systems and Disruptions in Food Supply Chain. *International Journal of Production Research, Ahead-of-Print* (https://doi.org/10.1080/00207543.2020.1792000), 1–16.

Solms, R. v., & Niekerk, J. v. (2013). From Information Security to Cyber Security. *Computers & Security, 38*(1), 97–102.

Şeker, M., & Bulduklu, Y. (2018). Kurum Kültürü ve Değerler. M. Şeker, Y. Bulduklu, & B. D. (Eds.), *Kurumlarda Değerler.* Konya: Necmettin Erbakan Üniversitesi Kültür Yayınları.

T.C. Sanayi ve Teknoloji Bakanlığı. (2018). *Türkiye'nin Sanayi Devrimi "Dijital Türkiye" Yol Haritasi.* Accessed September 2020. Güney Marmara Kalkınma Ajansı: https://www.gmka.gov.tr/dokumanlar/yayinlar/2023_Dijital-Turkiye-Yol-Haritasi.pdf.

Twinn, I., Qureshi, N., Conde, M. L., Guinea, C. G., Rojas, D. P., Luo, J., & Gupta, H. (2020). *The Impact of COVID-19 on Logistics.* International Finance Corporation (IFC).

Ünal, A. N., & Ergen, A. (2018). Siber Uzayda Yeterince Güvenli Davraniyor Muyuz? Istanbul Ilinde Yürütülen Nicel bir Araştirma. *MCBÜ Sosyal Bilimler Dergisi, 16*(2), 191–216.

Ünlü, D. E. (2020, February 03). *Geleceğe yatırımın yolu dijital dönüşüm.* Accessed September 2020, Dünya Gazetesi: https://www.dunya.com/kose-yazisi/gelecege-yatirimin-yolu-dijital-donusum/461690.

Ünsar, A., İnan, A., & Yürük, P. (2010). Çalişma Hayatinda Motivasyon ve Kişiyi Motive Eden Faktörler: Bir Alan Araştirmasi. *Trakya Üniversitesi Sosyal Bilimler Dergisi, 12*(1), 248–262.

Urciuoli, L., Mannistto, T., Hintsa, J., & Khan, T. (2013). Supply Chain Cyber Security – Potential Threats. *Information & Security: An International Journal, 29*(1), 51–68.

UTİKAD. (2017, March 14). *Ulaştirma Sektörü Siber Güvenlikte Geride Kaliyor.* Accessed September 2019. UTIKAD: https://www.utikad.org.tr/Detay/Sektor-Haberleri/14625/ulastirma-sektoru-siber-guvenlikte-geride-kaliyor-.

Villani, E., & Greco, L. (2018). The Dark Side of Outsourcing: The Case of Logistics. In M. F. (Eds.), *Positive and Negative Aspects of Outsourcing.* Croatia: InTech.

Wickham Heath Consulting. (2018). *Cross-Border Data Flows Realising Benefits and Removing Barriers.* GSMA.

Wisetjindawat, W., Burke, M. I., & Fujita, M. (2017). Analysing Impacts of Natural Disasters on Logistics Activities: Flood Risks and Petroleum Fuels in Queensland, Australia. *World Conference on Transport Research-WCTR 2016* (1197–1212). Shanghai: Transportation Research Procedia Vol. 25.

World Economic Forum. (2016). *Digital Transformation of Industries Logistics Industry.* Geneva: World Economic Forum.

World Economic Forum. (2018). *Delivering the Goods: E-commerce Logistics Transformation.* Geneva: World Economic Forum.

Yıldız, H., Yıldız, B., & Ateş, H. (2015). Sanal Kaytarma Davranışlarının Sergirilmesinde Örgütsel Adalet Algısının Rolü Var Mıdır. *Bilgi Ekonomisi ve Yönetimi Dergisi, 10*(2), 55–66.

Yankın, F. B. (2019). Dijital Dönüşüm Sürecinde Çalişma Yaşami. *Trakya Üniversitesi İktisadi ve İdari Bilimler Fakültesi E-Dergi, 7*(2), 1–38.

www.ingramcontent.com/pod-product-compliance
Ingram Content Group UK Ltd.
Pitfield, Milton Keynes, MK11 3LW, UK
UKHW021014120926
8556IPUK00040B/1145

9 783631 831106